KU-063-700

Contents

A Nazi Party poster: 'Yes! Leader, we will follow you!' But not all Germans were completely loyal to the Nazi regime and opposition ranged from minor to major activities.

Introduction

This book examines opposition and resistance towards the Nazi regime from 1933 to 1945. It must be stressed at the beginning of this study that most Germans were loyal to Hitler's regime. Hitler was a dictator whose popularity with the German people grew as unemployment fell in the mid 1930s and when the Nazi regime went from success to success in foreign policy from 1936 to 1942. Of course, there remained a substantial number of Germans who were coerced into a reluctant acceptance of the regime. The Nazi regime was not destroyed by a popular uprising from within Germany but by the efforts of the military personnel of the Allies, led by the Soviet Union, America and Britain.

In fact, active resistance against Nazism was undertaken by less than 1 per cent of the German population. Resistance to Nazi rule from 1933 to 1945 was undertaken by small groups whose activities were easily detected by the Nazi police authorities. Of course, this low level of resistance and opposition was to some degree restricted by the repressive nature of the Nazi state. Everyone who lived under Nazi rule knew that open resistance ran the real risk of imprisonment and even death. At the very least, opponents risked losing their jobs or being informed upon to the Nazi authorities. The repressive nature of the Nazi regime meant that most Germans, especially those who had not been Nazis before 1933, were extremely cautious about making comments critical of the regime in public.

Unlike members of the French resistance, who fought against an occupying power and were able to find shelter almost everywhere, the opposite was true of those who resisted the Nazi regime. The opponents of the Nazis were fighting against a national government. As a result, opponents were regarded as traitors by the majority of the German people, especially during wartime, when German patriotism was at its height. It is worth adding that it was the supply of information by 'loyal' Germans which helped the Gestapo to track down many of those engaged in the underground resistance. Hence, the repressive nature of the Nazi regime, combined with the loyalty of those Germans who supported it, ensured that a popular and co-ordinated resistance movement never existed within Germany. Resistance to Nazi rule, therefore, had no popular backing, or widespread support.

This book examines the lonely world of those individuals and groups who did offer resistance and opposition to the Nazi regime. It will be emphasised throughout that there were different levels of resistance to Nazism, starting at the bottom with mild forms of nonconformist behaviour such as refusal to give the Nazi salute, listening to the BBC and telling anti-Hitler jokes, moving upwards towards opposition activities such as refusing to join the Hitler Youth, going on strike and protesting in public against the regime, up to the highest levels of outright resistance such as attempting to assassinate Hitler or organising a coup to overthrow the Nazi regime.

All these differing varieties and levels of opposition and resistance to the Nazi regime will be examined in the chapters which follow. In Chapter 1, the opposition and resistance activities of Social Democrats, Communists and industrial workers are explored. Chapter 2 examines the protest of youth against the rigid conformity of Nazi society. In Chapter 3, the protest by the students of the White Rose group in Munich is evaluated. Chapter 4 explores the opposition to Nazi policies from the Christian churches. In Chapter 5, the spotlight is placed on those conservatives, generals and aristocrats, drawn from the elite of German society, who opposed the Nazi regime. Chapter 6 examines the failed attempt by Claus von Stauffenberg to murder Hitler on 20 July 1944. In Chapter 7, the concluding chapter, the changing historical debate over resistance and opposition in Nazi Germany is critically assessed.

This is the story of a few brave individuals, located in a wide variety of small groups, who attempted to oppose and resist Nazi tyranny. It is an account of those Germans who decided to fight against Hitler, most of whom were eventually caught by the Nazis and executed. It is a story of tragic failure, but one which reveals that not all Germans were seduced by the charismatic power of Adolf Hitler.

Opposition and resistance from Social Democrats, Communists and industrial workers

The three largest groups participating in resistance against the Nazi regime were the Social Democrats, Communists and industrial workers. The Social Democratic Party (SPD) was banned in 1933 along with all other political parties, but its exiled leadership and activists inside Germany continued to oppose the Nazi regime. A much greater level of active resistance to Nazi rule was offered by the Communist Party (KPD), which undertook extensive underground resistance against Nazism after its suppression in 1933. Industrial workers were a third group to offer resistance to the Nazi regime.

Social Democratic opposition

Before 1933, the SPD was supported by a million members and five million voters, located primarily in working-class areas. When Hitler gained power, the SPD organised anti-Nazi demonstrations. In March 1933, SPD members of the Reichstag (the German parliament) bravely voted against the Enabling Act, the law which gave Hitler unlimited constitutional power. In May 1933, the funds of the party were seized. In June 1933, the SPD was forced to disband. With all avenues of legal opposition closed off, the leadership of the SPD fled into exile, residing in Prague (1933–37), Paris (1937–40) and eventually in London (1940–45).

The SPD quickly established a very sophisticated underground organisation to oppose the Nazi regime, consisting of the exiled leadership, newspapers and party activists. A very important SPD resistance group was known as Red Shock Troop (Roter Stosstrupp), which was on the socialist fringe of the party. By the end of 1933, the group had 3,000 members, consisting primarily of university students based in the Berlin area. The group set up a newspaper called *The Red Shock Troop* (*Der rote Stosstrupp*), which appeared every 10 days. The editorials of the newspaper constantly suggested that the Nazi regime would be overthrown by the revolutionary action of German workers. In December 1933, however, the leaders of Red Shock Troop were arrested by the Gestapo (the Nazi secret police) and imprisoned in a concentration camp.

Nevertheless, the SPD's Berlin regional committee took part in a number of other resistance activities against the Nazi regime between 1934 and 1937. Using funds supplied by the exiled SPD leadership, a newspaper entitled *Socialist Action* (*Sozialistische Aktion*) was circulated widely throughout Berlin. In January 1935, however, the Gestapo arrested the leaders of the committee. By the end of 1938, the continued success of the Gestapo in finding and arresting SPD underground resistance groups led the exiled SPD leadership to conclude that underground resistance activities, including the production of anti-Nazi pamphlets and newspapers, were too dangerous and so they were ended.

From 1939, therefore, the remaining SPD activists concentrated their efforts on collecting information on the state of public opinion in Nazi Germany. The reports produced by SPD local secretariats (known as the SOPADE reports) revealed that, while most Germans had been won over to supporting the Nazi regime, most Social Democrats had reluctantly accepted the Nazi regime as a 'fact of life' and had turned inward, towards the home and the family.[1]

Overall, the SPD came to accept there was no way of overthrowing a powerful and repressive totalitarian regime, supported by a strong police force and the majority of the people, by undertaking underground propaganda. As a result, the SPD leadership came to the conclusion that the Nazi regime could be overthrown only by a coup led by the German army.

New Beginning

On the left of the SPD, a very small fringe group known as New Beginning (Neu Beginnen) also engaged in resistance activities. The group took its name from a pamphlet written in 1932 by Walter Löwenheim (using the pseudonym 'Miles'). The members of New Beginning met secretly in private houses and flats to discuss what the future direction of German politics might be. The leaders of New Beginning believed that left-wing disunity was one of the key reasons why Hitler had come to power. As a result, the group felt a left-wing coalition, consisting of Social Democrats and Communists, was the best means of combating Nazism. Yet the SPD leadership dismissed the idea because they felt that the Communists' desire for a 'dictatorship of the proletariat' was incompatible with the Social Democratic desire for a democratic government based on free elections.

During 1935, a number of the most active members of New Beginning were arrested by the Gestapo. Yet the group, in a much depleted form, continued to operate. In the autumn of 1938, New Beginning was decimated by a further wave of arrests by the Gestapo. The reason why the group survived for so long was because its members had attempted to conduct their opposition through discussions in private.

Communist resistance groups

The KPD and groups associated with it led the underground resistance against the Nazi regime. However, the Communists who resisted Nazism faced a multitude of dangers, and most died in the struggle. From 1933 to 1939, 150,000 Communists were detained in Nazi concentration camps and a further 30,000 were executed.[2]

A photomontage by John Heartfield, which appeared in the Communist magazine *AIZ*. Heartfield had changed his name from Helmut Herzfeld in 1916 as a protest against the extreme nationalism in Germany at the time. This poster was produced shortly after the Reichstag fire in 1933 when the Nazis blamed Communists for starting the blaze. Heartfield is clearly pointing to Hermann Göring as the real culprit.

The Nazi attack on the KPD

The German Communist Party, set up in 1919, had been the largest (outside the Soviet Union) before 1933. The strongest areas of Communist electoral strength were Berlin, Hamburg, Stuttgart, Leipzig, the industrial areas of the Ruhr and Saxony. When Hitler was appointed Chancellor on 30 January 1933, the largest street demonstrations against his new regime were led by Communists.

However, the KPD was the first organisation to experience the full vigour of Nazi terror. The burning of the Reichstag (allegedly started by a young Dutch Communist, Marinus van der Lubbe) on 27 February 1933 provided the Nazi regime with an ideal excuse to step up its persecution of Communists. On 6 March 1933 (the day after the last democratic election in Nazi Germany), the activities of the KPD were declared illegal. The party's leaders assumed that Hitler's regime, which they dubbed a 'puppet of big business and the army', would soon run into political and economic difficulties, thereby paving the way for a Communist revolution. This proved a fatal error of judgement.

In a matter of weeks after Hitler came to power, the Nazi regime eagerly set about the task of destroying the KPD as a political force. Nazi blackshirts (that is the SS, the Nazi Party's special security force) launched a series of daring and brutal raids on the working-class suburbs of major German cities, during which duplicating machines, typewriters and propaganda material were seized. The aim of these raids was to demoralise Communists and to deter them from mounting resistance. Pro-Communist newspapers were closed down and thousands of Communists were carted off to concentration camps. Of course, members of the KPD had expected Nazi brutality, but not on anything like such a scale. It soon became clear that the Nazi regime had inflicted a major defeat on Communism in Germany. Those leaders of the KPD who were not arrested by the Nazis fled into exile to Prague, then to Paris and finally ended up in Moscow after 1941.

After 1933, therefore, the KPD was forced to change from a mass party with 360,000 members into a clandestine anti-Nazi underground organisation. However, those Communists brave enough to engage in the resistance against the Nazi regime faced a lonely, hopeless struggle, followed by the inevitable knock on the door from a member of the Gestapo, detention in a concentration camp and, in most cases, execution.

The extent of Communist resistance

It is difficult to establish the exact extent of Communist resistance, but the following figures offer a rough guide. In the summer of 1933, 50 per cent of KPD members still paid contributions to the party. In 1933, the Berlin Supreme Court heard 1,000 cases concerning resistance activities brought against members of the KPD.[3] One estimate suggests that between 1933 and 1935 around 10 per cent of KPD members (some 36,000 people) were active within the underground resistance. In 1935, the Gestapo estimated there were 5,000 active members of the Communist resistance in Berlin alone. Most of those involved in the Communist resistance were of two predominant types: skilled members of the working class, operating in factories, and unemployed workers living in inner-city areas.

The activities of the Communist resistance

The most important activity of the Communist underground was the distribution of anti-Nazi literature. Communist leaflets and newspapers were circulated in beer halls and workplaces in working-class areas. The leading Communist newspaper, *Red Flag* (*Rote Fahne*), and a number of regional Communist newspapers were printed and distributed widely throughout Germany from 1933 to 1935. In the same period, the KPD produced and distributed over a million anti-Nazi leaflets. A great deal of this literature focused on the brutal acts of terror undertaken by the Nazi authorities against members of the working class. According to Gestapo reports, 1.2 million Communist anti-Nazi pamphlets were seized in 1934, and 1.67 million were discovered by the Nazi authorities in 1935.[4]

The underground network of the KPD

The maintenance of an extensive underground network required a major organisational effort. The key posts within the Communist resistance were filled by paid party activists, who were supported by illegal subscriptions collected in factories and working-class areas. These Communist activists used false names and forged papers. The chief aim of a member of the Communist underground was to keep one step ahead of the Gestapo. This proved an increasingly difficult task. Indeed, most Communist activists did not elude the Gestapo for more than six months. Of the 422 people who had been salaried KPD officials in January 1933, 219 had been arrested, 125 were in exile, 24 had been killed by the Nazis and 54 had left the party by the end of 1935. The number of Communists arrested by the Gestapo for resistance activities fell from 14,000 in 1935 to 3,800 in 1938.[5]

The KPD rethinks its strategy

In the late 1930s, as Hitler moved from victory to victory in foreign policy and unemployment fell, many workers became reluctantly resigned to accepting the Nazi regime as a fact of life. A large section of the working class had not been won over to Hitler's regime, but had been effectively neutralised as a real danger to the survival of the regime.

By the late 1930s the underground Communist resistance network had been greatly reduced by the activities of the Gestapo. As a result, the exiled leadership of the KPD decided to rethink the tactics of resistance. At the Berne Conference, convened in January 1939, the exiled KPD leadership undertook a major policy review, which resulted in a demand for the creation of a 'Popular Front' consisting of all anti-fascist forces inside and outside Germany.

In August 1939, however, this policy suffered a severe setback when Stalin's Communist Soviet Union signed a non-aggression pact with Hitler's Nazi Germany. The KPD leadership (a close ally of Stalin's regime) called for 'observance' of the Nazi–Soviet pact but continued to warn of the consequences of Nazi aggression.

The growth of Communist resistance after the invasion of the Soviet Union

It was in the period following the invasion of the Soviet Union on 22 June 1941 that Communist resistance revived. Indeed, the number of anti-Nazi leaflets seized by the Gestapo in 1941 grew from 62 in January to 10,227 in October. During the same period, a number of important underground Communist groups, not officially connected to the KPD but sympathetic towards it, began to engage in resistance activities. They operated in a number of German cities and factories.

The Uhrig group

The Uhrig group, led by Robert Uhrig, operated during 1941 and 1942 in Berlin, with about 100 active members. The Uhrig group took the view that the Soviet Union, the only Communist state in Europe, must be defended from Nazi aggression at all costs. To support this view, the Uhrig group flyposted billboards throughout Berlin with anti-Nazi slogans urging workers to engage in sabotage. In September 1941, the group won support from 70 workers based in a large Berlin arms factory (the Deutsche Waffen- und Munitionsfabrik). The Uhrig group also produced a monthly news sheet called *Information Service*

(*Informationsdienst*), which gave news of 'the true military situation in the Soviet Union' and publicised Nazi war crimes.

The Uhrig group wanted to weaken German public support for the war against the Soviet Union. However, Uhrig and over 200 supporters of his group were arrested by the Gestapo in February 1942 and 100 of them were subsequently executed. This was a severe blow to Communist resistance in the Berlin area. Even so, 67 separate factory groups closely connected with the Uhrig group continued to engage in resistance activities.

Home Front

Another Communist resistance group worthy of mention is Home Front (Innere Front), located in the Berlin and Hamburg areas. The leading figures in Home Front (Wilhelm Guddorf, John Sieg, Martin Weise and Jon Graudenz) had all been active members of the KPD before 1933. In fact, many of them had been on the editorial staff of *Red Flag*. In 1941, Home Front produced a fortnightly anti-Nazi underground newspaper described as 'a fighting sheet for a new, free Germany', which aimed to 'expose the lies of Nazi propaganda'. This newspaper was circulated in a number of factories in Berlin. Home Front also produced a number of anti-Nazi pamphlets highlighting Nazi war crimes on the eastern front.

Home Front was made up of well-educated KPD members and drew support from like-minded Marxist intellectuals and professionals. However, its propaganda activities quickly came to the attention of the Gestapo. In the autumn of 1942, several members of Home Front were arrested, including Guddorf and Sieg.

The Red Orchestra

Another group of Communists who also engaged in resistance activities was dubbed by the Gestapo the Red Orchestra (Rote Kapelle). It was led by Arvid Harnack and Harro Schulze-Boysen. The members of this group had not been members of the KPD, but they were generally sympathetic to Communism and the Soviet Union. The main activity of the Red Orchestra was passing on secrets of the German war effort to the Soviet government. This was possible because many of the members of the Red Orchestra were employed in the Nazi ministries concerned with the economy and the air-force. The Gestapo eventually discovered the identities of the leading members of this group, who were put on trial and executed.

The Baum group

The Baum group (named after its leader, Herbert Baum) consisted of around 30 pro-Communist Jews, aged between 20 and 30, all of whom worked at the Siemens plant in Berlin. The Baum group produced a monthly news sheet entitled *The Way Out* (Der Ausweg), which described itself as a 'paper of the anti-fascist struggle'. The group urged German soldiers to 'fight with us for the overthrow of the Hitler regime'.[6]

The most daring act carried out by the Baum group was to break into an anti-Soviet exhibition, organised by the Ministry of Propaganda, on 18 May 1942 and set fire to a number of exhibits. Within days of this incident, the Gestapo rounded up all the members of the Baum group, who were subjected to appalling torture before they were executed. In a further act of reprisal against the group, the Nazis arrested 500 Berlin-based Jews, who had no connection with the Baum group, and executed them.[7]

The revival of KPD activity

The destruction of most of the Communist anti-Nazi groups by the Gestapo during 1942 was a severe blow. Indeed, the crackdown on the Communist resistance by the Nazi authorities was unrelenting. However, the defeat of the German army at Stalingrad in February 1943 led to a revival of resistance activities by the KPD leadership, exiled in Moscow.

The National Committee for a Free Germany

The KPD set up the National Committee for a Free Germany (Nationalkomitee Freies Deutschland), which used a large radio transmitter (donated by Stalin) to broadcast directly to the German people, using the title Radio Free Germany. The broadcasts of Radio Free Germany urged all Germans to turn against the Nazi regime and promised that a post-Hitler Germany would be based on democratic ideas. The Committee also established a newspaper, *Free Germany* (*Freies Deutschland*), edited by Anton Ackermann, a member of the exiled KPD leadership. The National Committee for a Free Germany gave encouragement to resistance fighters to unite against the Nazi regime.

The last months

The crackdown against KPD figures intensified still further after the 1944 bomb attack on Hitler. On 18 August 1944, Ernst Thälmann, the KPD leader before his arrest in 1933, was executed in Buchenwald concentration camp, along with 24 former Communist Reichstag deputies. Even during the latter stages of the war, members of the Communist resistance were still hunted down by the Gestapo, and many were arrested and executed. Members of the Communist resistance, facing denunciation by their fellow citizens, had nowhere to run and nowhere to hide from the searchlights of the Gestapo.

It is only in recent years, with the ending of the Cold War, that full credit is finally being afforded to the brave heroes and heroines of the Communist resistance against Nazism. In spite of all the danger, Communist resistance never ceased inside Nazi Germany, which is a testimony to the self-sacrifice Communists were willing to endure in their desire to rid Germany of Nazi tyranny.

Resistance by industrial workers

There are also numerous examples of resistance from industrial workers. This took a variety of forms, including absenteeism from work, sabotage of industrial machinery, the refusal to serve in the German army and to give the Hitler salute. Gestapo records show widespread worker protests over rises in food prices in

1935. There is also evidence of strikes by workers who built the motorways in the mid 1930s and many examples of deliberate slow working in armaments factories.

The most remarkable attempt by an individual worker to bring down the Nazi regime was undertaken by Georg Elser, a joiner from Württemberg. Elser had always voted for the KPD in elections and was aggrieved over the destruction of workers' rights by the Nazi regime. On 8 November 1939, he planted a bomb in a Munich beer hall at which Hitler was due to give a speech. However, due to bad weather and good luck, Hitler's plane to Munich was delayed and he arrived late for his speech. In fact, the bomb Elser had planted exploded at the exact time when Hitler would have been speaking if he had arrived on time. Elser was arrested and subsequently executed for attempting to assassinate the Nazi leader.[8]

A more organised form of opposition to the Nazi regime was undertaken by factory workers (based in Hamburg and many other industrial towns in central Germany), most of whom were sympathetic to the KPD. Towards the end of the war industrial unrest greatly increased. From January to the end of June 1944, for example, 193,024 foreign workers were arrested for taking part in strikes. Even so, the much hoped for 'workers' uprising' did not take place.

Hamburg 1936. Shipyard workers giving the Hitler salute as a ship is launched. One man in the crowd risked arrest, imprisonment or death by keeping his arms folded as a gesture of defiance.

In many German industrial areas there is evidence of workers engaging in resistance activity. In Dortmund prison, for example, of the 21,833 prisoners serving time for political opposition to the Nazi regime, the overwhelming majority recorded their occupation as 'industrial worker'. The same is true of the prison records of other penal institutions in Germany during the Nazi era.[9] Most of the factory workers who engaged in resistance against the Nazis either were members of, or had sympathy towards, the KPD.

The Anti-Fascist Workers' Group of Central Germany

One of the most organised factory groups was known as the Anti-Fascist Workers' Group of Central Germany. This group engaged in acts of sabotage and passed on information to workers, gained by illegally listening to broadcasts made by the BBC. The members of this group were arrested in a series of Gestapo raids in late August 1944.

The Mannheim group

Another leading factory group which engaged in anti-Nazi propaganda was known as the Mannheim group, based in the Rhineland area. This group produced a monthly newspaper called *The Herald* (*Der Verbote*), which first appeared in October 1942. The Gestapo found a copy of this newspaper and arrested most of the leaders of the group in March 1943.

Document case study

Opposition and resistance from Social Democrats, Communists and industrial workers

1.1 The problems of opposition – a report from a Social Democrat, 1934

The weakness of the Opposition is the strength of the regime. Its opponents are ideologically and organizationally weak. They are ideologically weak because the great mass are only discontented, they are merely grumblers whose discontent springs from economic motives. That is probably true of the Mittelstand [middle class] and of the peasantry. The loudest and strongest criticism comes from these groups, but the criticism springs from selfish interest. These groups are least prepared to fight seriously against the regime because they have the least idea of what they should be fighting for . . . Its opponents are organizationally weak because it is of the essence of a fascist system that it does not allow its opponents to organize collectively.

Source: J. Noakes and G. Pridham (eds.), *Nazism 1919–1945, vol. 2: State, economy and society 1933–1939*, Exeter, 1984, pp. 579–80

1.2 Communist resistance – an underground Communist pamphlet, Berlin, May 1942

. . . the Hitler gang and their root, the monopoly capitalist mob, who bear the sole guilt for and are the beneficiaries of the war, must be overthrown by a true popular revolution, expropriated and rendered harmless for ever so that our people cannot be plunged into war for a third time, but that the preconditions can be created for building a new, free Germany. The sooner our people carry out this deed the lesser will be the national catastrophe; the nations which have been attacked by Hitler will, thereby, recognize that the German people and Hitler are not identical with Hitler and his crimes and, instead of exacting revenge, they will extend to us the hand of brotherhood, grant us a just peace and treat us like a nation with equal rights. But woe betide our nation if it does not take part in the destruction of the Hitler beast . . . For Hitler, fascism is war without end and the victory of the Red Army [the army of the Soviet Union] over Hitler's Wehrmacht [the German army] will bring Germany an immediate and just peace. Thus the military defeat of Hitler and his fall are vital for Germany. And it is the duty of every German to help energetically to achieve this goal without delay.

Source: J. Noakes (ed.), *Nazism 1919–1945: a documentary reader, vol. 4: The German home front in World War II*, Exeter, 1998, p. 587

1.3 Guidelines for working in the underground Communist resistance – a Communist pamphlet, 1941

The most important principles for our illegal activity must be reliability, punctuality and caution. Anyone who sins against these three commandments not only jeopardizes himself but all our work . . . Meetings in comrades' flats should be avoided if possible since experience has shown that the blocks are often under surveillance. One should not go straight from home to a meeting place but take a roundabout route in order to spot anyone who may be following. Our organization will only be based on factory cells which should not contain more than three people. Only workers who have proved reliable should be admitted to these cells. Gossips and those partial to alcohol are to be excluded from party work on principle. Inquisitiveness and boastfulness have no place in the party.

Source: Noakes (ed.), *Nazism 1919–1945, vol. 4*, p. 587

1.4 The final letter of a Communist to his father, before execution by the Nazi regime for resistance activities, May 1943

My dear Father

Be strong! I am dying as I lived: as a fighter in the class war. It is easy to call yourself a Communist as long as you don't have to shed blood for it. You only show whether you really are one when the hour comes when you have to prove yourself. I am one, father . . . The war won't last much longer and then your hour will have come. Think of all those who have already travelled down this road that I must go down today and will still have to travel down it and learn one thing from the Nazis; every weakness will have to be paid for with . . . blood. So be merciless! Remain hard! . . . Oh father, dear father, you dear and good man! If only I did not have to fear that you will collapse under the shock of my death. Be tough, tough, tough! Prove that you have been a whole-hearted life-long fighter in the class struggle. Help him, Frieda, raise his spirits. He must not be allowed to succumb. His life does not belong to him but to the movement! Now, a thousand times more than ever before.

Source: Noakes (ed.), *Nazism 1919–1945, vol. 4*, pp. 588–89

1.5 'Why I tried to assassinate the Führer' – the statement of Georg Elser, 1939

After reaching voting age, I always voted for the KPD [Communist Party] party list because I thought it was a workers' party which certainly supports the workers. But I never became a member of this party because I thought it was enough if I voted for it. I never took part in any actions such as distributing leaflets, demonstrations or graffiti . . . In my opinion the conditions of the workers have deteriorated in various respects since the nation's [Nazi] revolution. For example, I have noticed that wages have been getting lower and deductions getting higher . . . Furthermore, in my view, since the national revolution the workers are under a certain amount of restraint. For example, workers can no longer change their jobs when they want and nowadays, as a result of the HJ [Hitler Youth], they are no longer in charge of their children. And in the religious sphere too they are no longer as free as they were . . . The discontent among the workers which I had observed since 1933 and the war I thought was unavoidable since autumn 1938 [the time of the crisis over the Sudetenland] preoccupied my thoughts. I simply started thinking about how one could improve the conditions of the workers and avoid a war . . . The result of my deliberations was that conditions in Germany could only be improved by removing the current leadership . . . If I'm asked whether I consider the deed I have done as a sin within the meaning of Protestant doctrine then I would have to say no! . . . After all, through my deed [the attempt to assassinate Hitler] I wanted to prevent more blood being spilled.

Source: Noakes (ed.), *Nazism 1919–1945, vol. 4*, pp. 592–94

Document case-study questions

1 What insights does 1.1 provide into the difficulties faced by Social Democrats who engaged in resistance activities?

2 What does 1.2 tell us about the attitude of the Communist resistance towards the Nazi regime?

3 What does 1.3 tell us about the difficulties faced by Communist members of the resistance?

4 What conclusions can be drawn from 1.4 about the reasons why this Communist fought against the Nazi regime?

5 What insights does 1.5 provide about Elser's motivation for trying to assassinate Hitler?

Notes and references

1 K. von Klemperer, *German resistance against Hitler*, Oxford, 1992, pp. 60–62. See also W. Allen, 'Social Democratic resistance against Hitler and the European tradition of underground movements', in F. Nicosia and L. Stokes (eds.), *Germans against Nazism: nonconformity, opposition and resistance in the Third Reich*, Oxford, 1990, pp. 191–204.

2 For a detailed study of Communist resistance against Nazism, see A. Merson, *Communist resistance in Nazi Germany*, London, 1985.

3 H. Graml, H. Mommsen, H-J. Reich and E. Wolf, *The German resistance to Hitler*, London, 1970, p. 169.

4 Merson, *Communist resistance*, p. 116.

5 *Ibid.*, pp. 182–83.

6 *Ibid.*, p. 243.

7 For a detailed analysis of Jewish resistance, see K. Jonca, 'Jewish resistance to Nazi racial legislation in Silesia 1933–1937', in Nicosia and Stokes (eds.), *Germans against Nazism*, pp. 77–86.

8 See J. Noakes (ed.), *Nazism 1919–1945, vol. 4: The German home front in World War II*, Exeter, 1998, pp. 592–95.

9 I. Kershaw, *The Nazi dictatorship: problems and perspectives of interpretation*, 3rd edn, London, 1993, p. 172.

2 Youth protest

Most young people in Germany from 1933 to 1945 were loyal members of either the Hitler Youth (Hitler Jugend, for boys) or the German Girls' League (Bund deutscher Mädel). These organisations attempted to control every aspect of the leisure time of German youth and encouraged unhesitating support for Hitler and the Nazi regime. In March 1939, it became compulsory for all young people to join.

However, it would be wrong to believe the Nazi regime succeeded in winning over the entire youth of Germany. There were some young people who strongly objected to rigid indoctrination and discipline, preferring instead to form nonconformist youth groups and gangs who engaged in acts of protest and defiance towards the Nazi regime. The two most significant youth groups in Germany during the Nazi era were the 'Edelweiss Pirates' (Edelweisspiraten) and 'Swing Youth' (Swing Jugend).[1]

The Edelweiss Pirates

The Edelweiss Pirates emerged during the late 1930s, located in the working-class districts of a number of west German towns, most notably Cologne, Düsseldorf, Essen, Wuppertal and Duisburg. The Pirates consisted primarily of 12–18-year-old boys who had no distinctive political ideology but great antipathy towards the grim uniformity of the Hitler Youth and the general lack of freedom in Nazi Germany. In order to stress their free-spirited individuality, and quite natural desire for youthful rebellion against authority, the Edelweiss Pirates wore distinctive checked shirts, which sported a metal badge with an edelweiss flower emblazoned upon it, dark short trousers, a windcheater, a scarf and flashy white socks. The very few girls who joined wore windcheaters, white sweaters and white socks. Many members of the group had much longer hair than was the norm for young people in Nazi Germany at the time. The local Gestapo compiled lists of the fashions worn by the Edelweiss Pirates in order to identify and arrest them. The Edelweiss Pirates were closely related to a number of other subversive youth gangs, such as the 'Raving Dudes', based in Essen, and the 'Navajos', who operated in Cologne. These youth groups also wore checked shirts with either an edelweiss or a skull badge.

The Edelweiss Pirates appear to have grown spontaneously, as a youthful rebellion against the rigid control of the Hitler Youth over German teenagers. Most of them had never joined the Hitler Youth or had left it. One of the chief

15

The public execution of a group of *Edelweisspiraten* in Cologne, 1944.

slogans used by the Edelweiss Pirates in street graffiti was 'Eternal War on the Hitler Youth'. They operated in small local gangs. In the inner-city areas they congregated on street corners, hung around parts of the city centre or met in local parks. It was difficult for the Nazi authorities to distinguish their behaviour from less politically challenging forms of juvenile delinquency. It seems the young people who joined the Edelweiss Pirates had grown sick of the lack of freedom which the Nazi regime had imposed on German society.

To break free from Nazi discipline, the Edelweiss Pirates went on long hikes, carrying rucksacks. They engaged in camping trips during wartime, when the Nazi regime had placed severe limitations on travel. Once they had pitched their tents, the Edelweiss Pirates would sing extremely funny parodies of Hitler Youth songs and tell each other 'dirty jokes' about the sexual activities of the Hitler Youth. The Gestapo believed that the Edelweiss Pirates engaged in under-age sex orgies on these camping trips, but there is no evidence to suggest that the sexual activity of the Edelweiss Pirates was any higher than that of similar 14–18-year-olds in Nazi Germany.

It was during the war years (1939–45), with a reduction in parental supervision and the severe disruption to local leisure facilities caused by increased Allied bombing raids, that the 'subversive' activities of the Edelweiss Pirates grew markedly. In the cities, they took part in pitched battles with members of the Hitler Youth and daubed subways with anti-Nazi slogans such as 'Down with Hitler – We Want Freedom', 'Medals for Murder' and 'Down with Nazi Brutality'. In addition, the Edelweiss Pirates posted the anti-Nazi leaflets dropped by British and American bombers through the letter boxes of local people. Towards the end of the Second World War, with Germany heading for defeat, many of the Edelweiss Pirates bravely shielded army deserters and joined with other resistance fighters, especially Communists, to engage in many acts of industrial sabotage. These activities reveal how the youthful rebellion of the Edelweiss Pirates increasingly turned into active resistance against the Nazi regime.

The response of the Nazi authorities to the nonconformist activities of the Edelweiss Pirates was by no means uniform. In some areas, their activities were simply regarded by the local police force as childish pranks. However, during wartime, the Gestapo defined their activities as opposition and placed leaders of the Edelweiss Pirates under strict surveillance. The Gestapo regarded the Edelweiss Pirates as extremely hostile to the Hitler Youth and a growing danger to other young people in Germany. As a result, the Gestapo initiated a major crackdown against the Edelweiss Pirates. On 7 December 1942, 739 Pirates were arrested in Düsseldorf, Duisburg, Essen and Wuppertal. They were placed in a 're-education camp' designed to instil conformity towards Nazi ideas. In October 1944, the SS issued a decree on the 'combating of youth gangs', which led to further arrests of leading Edelweiss Pirates. In November 1944, the leaders of the Cologne Edelweiss Pirates were publicly hanged in order to deter other young people from joining the group.

The increasingly subversive activities of the Edelweiss Pirates justify their inclusion among the active 'resistance' against the Nazi regime. During the latter stages of the Second World War, they were fully aware that their activities carried the probability of arrest and even execution. However, the key motive behind the resistance activities of the Edelweiss Pirates was primarily a strong and normal youthful desire for personal liberty and independence. In essence, they wanted a more open and free society than existed within Nazi Germany, without having any set of clear political ideals of their own. They were rebels without a cause.[2]

Swing and Jazz Youth

There were other nonconformist youth groups which engaged in protests against the rigid cultural uniformity imposed by the Nazi regime. The two most significant groups in this category were known as 'Swing Youth' and 'Jazz Youth'. The nonconformist behaviour of these youth groups consisted of a powerful desire to listen to banned American music, in particular the swing music produced by big bands, such as the Glenn Miller Orchestra, and the American jazz music of the 1930s, made popular by leading performers such as Louis Armstrong. Heinrich Himmler, the leader of the SS, suggested that all young people who listened to jazz music should be 'beaten, given the severest exercise, and then put to hard labour'.[3]

Those associating with Swing Youth were predominantly teenagers from the affluent upper middle classes, located in big cities, most notably Berlin, Stuttgart, Hamburg, Kiel, Frankfurt and Dresden. They admired American music and popular culture and organised illegal dances, attended by up to 6,000 young people. The dances were characterised by what one Gestapo report described as 'an uninhibited indulgence in swing'.[4]

The members of Jazz Youth established illegal clubs at which 'hot jazz' was played. In Frankfurt, for example, the Gestapo closed down one jazz club called the Harlem Club. Members of Jazz and Swing Youth also set up their own swing and jazz big bands. The Gestapo closely monitored the activities of Swing and Jazz Youth during the war. Gestapo reports describe youths with long hair 'down to the collar', who loved to engage in an energetic dance, made popular in America in the 1930s, known as the 'jitterbug'.

In a move designed to clamp down on the nonconformist behaviour of Swing Youth, the Nazi regime imposed a ban in 1940 on public dances. Even so, members of Swing Youth were not deterred and organised private swing parties, while Jazz Youth created a number of illegal clubs, often located in the basement of large private houses.

It was the upper-middle-class affluence of members of Swing Youth which allowed them to purchase fashionable clothes, record players (known as gramophones) and illegal imports of American swing and jazz recordings. The Gestapo reports on swing groups also lay strong emphasis on the hedonistic pleasure which these uninhibited young Germans took in heavy drinking, sexual intercourse and high-energy dancing.

It seems the members of Swing and Jazz Youth were motivated, not by any burning desire to offer political resistance to the Nazi regime, but rather by a natural youthful desire to have a good time. As one member of the Swing Youth later recalled: 'We were not against the Nazis, but they were against us.'[5] These young people wanted a more open culture in Germany which would allow them to buy American swing and jazz music and to go to dance halls and jazz clubs in order to have a good time.[6]

The Nazi authorities interpreted the admiration shown by Swing and Jazz Youth for American culture as a lack of patriotism, when in reality it was the cultural freedom of America which they admired rather than its political organisation. It seems that a more culturally permissive society was what members of Swing Youth, who were usually located in cosmopolitan large cities, were primarily interested in.

Conclusions

The presence of these counter-cultural groups in Nazi Germany indicates that a very substantial minority of German youth, especially in the large German cities, remained indifferent and sometimes actively hostile to the rigidity of the Nazi state. The desire to express an individual cultural identity exhibited by these youth subcultures is further evidence that Nazism did not have the total grip on German society which its propaganda indicated. Indeed, these non-conformist activities show that the imposition of rigid discipline on German youth was beginning to break down even before the Nazi regime collapsed at the end of the Second World War.

Youth protest

2.1 The Edelweiss Pirates – a Nazi Party report, Düsseldorf, July 1943

Re: 'Edelweiss Pirates' . . . These adolescents, aged between 12 and 17, hang around late in the evening with musical instruments and young females. Since this riff raff is in large part outside the Hitler Youth and adopts a hostile attitude towards the organization, they represent a danger to other young people . . . There is a suspicion that it is these youths who have covered the walls of the pedestrian subway . . . with the slogans, 'Down with Hitler', 'Medals for Murder', 'Down with Nazi Brutality' etc. However often these inscriptions are removed, within a few days new ones appear on the walls.

Source: R. Bessel (ed.), *Life in the Third Reich*, Oxford, 1987, p. 34

2.2 The Edelweiss Pirates – a report by the Reich Ministry of Justice, 1944

The best-known politically hostile group are the Edelweiss Pirates. They organized in the West, namely in Cologne and Düsseldorf, but have subsequently spread over wide areas of the Reich. The Cologne juvenile court judge has recently described their external characteristics in a report. They wear the Edelweiss badge on or under the left lapel . . . The regulation uniform of the Edelweiss Pirates is short trousers, white socks, a check shirt, a white pullover and scarf and a windcheater . . . The boys belong mostly to the 14 to 18 year old age group . . . The leaders, in particular, who are tough and intelligent, come from previous leagues or from political parties . . . Most have an anti HJ [Hitler Youth] attitude, hate all discipline and thereby place themselves in opposition to the community. However, they are not only politically hostile (recently their attitude has reached the point of being hostile to the state) but as a result of their composition they are also criminal and antisocial, so that one cannot make a distinction between the two types of group.

Source: J. Noakes (ed.), *Nazism 1919–1945: a documentary reader, vol. 4: The German home front in World War II*, Exeter, 1998, pp. 450–52

2.3 A Swing Youth dance – a report from a member of the Hitler Youth, Hamburg, February 1940

The dance music was all English and American. Only swing dancing and jitterbugging took place. At the entrance to the hall stood a notice on which the words 'Swing prohibited' had been altered to 'Swing requested'. Without exception the participants accompanied the dances and songs by singing English lyrics . . . The dancers made an appalling sight. None of the couples danced normally; there was only swing of the worst sort. Sometimes two boys danced with one girl; sometimes several couples formed a circle, linking arms and jumping, slapping hands, even rubbing the backs of their heads together; and then, bent double, with the top half of the body hanging loosely down, long hair flapping into the face, they dragged themselves around practically on their knees. When the band played a rumba, the dancers went into wild ecstasy . . . The band played wilder and wilder numbers; none of the players were sitting any longer, they all 'jitterbugged' on the stage like wild animals.

Source: Bessel (ed.), *Life in the Third Reich*, p. 37

2.4 Swing Youth – a report by the Reich Ministry of Justice, 1944

(b) Liberal–individualistic gangs

They originated in north Germany, namely in Hamburg. The most striking example among these groups is the so-called Swing Youth, on whom there have been reports from various parts of the Reich . . . These groups are motivated by the desire to have a good time and have increasingly assumed a character bordering on criminal anti-social. Even before the war boys and girls from the socially privileged classes joined groups wearing strikingly casual clothes and became fans of English [American] music and dance. At the turn of 1939/40, the Flottbeck group organized dances which were attended by 5–6,000 people and were marked by an uninhibited indulgence in swing . . . The whole life style of these members costs a considerable amount of money . . . The greed to participate in what appeared to them to be a stylish life style in clubs, bars, cafes and house balls suppressed any positive attitude in responding to the needs of the time. They were unimpressed by the performance of our Wehrmacht [the German army]; those killed in action were held up to ridicule. An hostility to the war is clearly apparent . . . They regard Englishmen as the highest form of human development. A false conception of freedom leads them into opposition to the HJ.

Source: Noakes (ed.), *Nazism 1919–1945, vol. 4*, pp. 452–53

Document case-study questions

1 Explain briefly what is described in 2.1.

2 What does 2.2 tell us about how the Nazi authorities reacted to the Edelweiss Pirates?

3 What does 2.3 tell us about the attitude of the Nazis towards Swing Youth?

4 How does the Reich Ministry of Justice in 2.4 interpret the behaviour of Swing Youth?

Notes and references

1 For a detailed examination of the activities of Jazz and Swing Youth in Nazi Germany, see D. Peukert, *Inside Nazi Germany: conformity, opposition and racism in everyday life*, London, 1987.

2 D. Peukert, 'Youth in the Third Reich', in R. Bessel (ed.), *Life in the Third Reich*, Oxford, 1987, pp. 30–37.

3 A. Gill, *An honourable defeat: a history of German resistance to Hitler*, London, 1994, p. 195.

4 J. Noakes (ed.), *Nazism 1919–1945, vol. 4: The German home front in World War II*, Exeter, 1998, p. 452.

5 *Ibid.*

6 Peukert, 'Youth in the Third Reich', pp. 37–40.

Student protest: the White Rose

One of the most remarkable attempts to protest openly against the Nazi regime was undertaken by a brave group of university students. The focus of this student unrest was the University of Munich. The group was known as the White Rose (Die weisse Rose). Munich had special significance for the Nazis, as it was 'the birthplace of the Nazi Party'.[1]

The members of the White Rose

The White Rose consisted of five close friends based at the University of Munich – Hans and Sophie Scholl, Alexander Schmorell, Christoph Probst and Willi Graf – and Kurt Huber, Professor of Philosophy and Musicology at the University.

Hans Scholl

Hans Scholl was born on 21 September 1918 in Forchtenberg, a small town at the foot of the Alps. His father, Robert Scholl, was a liberal, free-thinking man, whose occupation was tax consultancy. His mother, Magdalene, was a liberal-minded Protestant lay preacher who brought up her children to have strong moral beliefs. Hans was an extrovert and impulsive child who loved outdoor pursuits. In 1933, Hans joined the Hitler Youth, even though his father was opposed to Nazism. In September 1935, Hans was selected by the Ulm branch of the Hitler Youth to carry the party flag at the annual Nazi Party rally in Nuremberg. However, the hate-filled speeches of Nazi leaders at the rally left Hans cold and when he returned home he promptly left the Hitler Youth. He soon became a member of the German Youth (Deutsche Jugend), a banned youth group, which was liberal, open-minded and very hostile to Nazism. In November 1937, Hans was arrested by the Gestapo because of his involvement with the German Youth. Indeed, he was held in youth custody for five weeks. Henceforth, the Gestapo reports branded the whole Scholl family as 'opponents' of the Nazi regime.

In 1939, Hans (having completed his period of conscription in the German army) started medical studies, beginning at the University of Göttingen, then moving to the University of Munich. During the early years of the Second World War, he was allowed to combine his medical studies with service in the army medical corps during university vacations. On the eastern front, Hans glimpsed, with great distress, the atrocities committed by the German army against Jews and Russian prisoners of war. These harrowing wartime experiences made him very determined to take part in resistance activities against the Nazi regime

Christoph Probst with Sophie and Hans Scholl, a picture taken in July 1942.

when he returned from army duties to resume his medical studies in the summer of 1942.

Sophie Scholl

Sophie Scholl, born on 9 May 1921, was the younger sister of Hans. In 1933, Sophie had joined the female equivalent of the Hitler Youth, the German Girls' League. However, free-spirited Sophie was never very enthusiastic about the German Girls' League and especially objected to the refusal of the organisation to allow her Jewish friends to become members. In November 1938, Sophie expressed great sadness when she heard news of *Kristallnacht* (the 'Night of the Broken Glass'), when Jews were openly attacked throughout Germany by members of the Nazi Party. In September 1939, Sophie expressed similar anger and disgust when she heard news of the outbreak of the Second World War.[2] In 1940, she embarked on a one-year course in nursery supervision, but in 1941 she was forced to undertake 'state work duty' (which involved some form of public service for girls and manual labour for boys), something which was compulsory for all students who intended to study at university. In May 1942, she started a degree in biology and philosophy at the University of Munich. On the day Sophie arrived at university, she was met by Hans at the local railway station. Not long afterwards, she decided to join the small group Hans had formed to engage in resistance activities against Nazi rule.

Alexander Schmorell

Alexander Schmorell was born on 3 September 1917. His father was a doctor. His mother, who died of typhoid when he was a child, was born in Russia. Alexander was never sympathetic towards Hitler and Nazism. Indeed, he retained strong emotional feelings and sympathy towards Russia and its people. In June 1941, Alexander was part of the German blitzkrieg attack which thrust with great speed through Russian territory. Alexander was greatly angered by the acts of extreme brutality against the Russian people that he witnessed on the eastern front. In the summer of 1942, he was granted leave by the army to study medicine at the University of Munich. On his arrival in Munich, he met Hans Scholl and soon agreed to engage in acts of resistance against the Nazi regime.

Christoph Probst

Christoph Probst, born on 6 November 1919, was Alexander Schmorell's best friend. Christoph led a very solitary and secluded existence during his childhood in a small town close to the Bavarian Alps. He suffered severe emotional upheaval due to the divorce of his parents. Christoph was indifferent towards Nazism but was drawn into the group because of his close friendship with Alexander. In 1939, he was called up for service in the Luftwaffe (the German air-force), but was allowed leave to study medicine at Innsbruck University, in Austria.

Willi Graf

Willi Graf, born on 2 January 1918, had a strict Catholic upbringing. During the 1930s he was a very active member of a banned anti-Nazi Catholic youth group, for which he was arrested in 1935 by the Gestapo. In 1939, he joined the German army as a medical orderly. In the summer of 1942, when he went to the University of Munich, Willi met the key figures in the White Rose and he was attracted to the idea of taking part in resistance activities against a Nazi regime which he believed had sought to undermine Christianity.

Kurt Huber

Kurt Huber was born on 24 October 1893. As a child, Kurt had contracted infantile paralysis and remained partly paralysed thereafter. Kurt was Professor of Philosophy and Musicology at the University of Munich and had written a definitive book on European folk songs. He was an inspirational and charismatic lecturer who often adopted a very critical attitude towards Nazism in his lectures. Kurt believed that Nazism was out to destroy the moral and cultural fabric of German society. Sophie Scholl attended Kurt's lectures and, sensing his hostility towards Hitlerism, she invited him to join the White Rose.

The ideas and activities of the White Rose

The five leading figures in the White Rose were motivated towards resistance primarily because of the lack of personal freedom in Nazi Germany. They wanted a post-Hitler Germany to be based on 'freedom of speech, freedom of confession' (i.e. religion) and the protection of all the citizens of Europe from 'arbitrary criminal power states'.[3]

The choice of the name 'White Rose' by the group has never been fully explained. The idea of a rose as a symbol of secrecy is one possible explanation. The use of a white rose may have been adopted in order to stress that members of the group were peaceful and not inspired by any recognised political colour. After all, the colour red was dominant in the flags of both the Communists and the Nazis. It has also been persuasively argued that the name 'White Rose' was taken from a novel popular in Germany during the 1930s of that title, written by B. Traven, which depicts a poor Mexican farmer fighting against the brutal and dictatorial practices of a large oil company.

The major aim of the White Rose was to influence the 'educated' sections of German public opinion to oppose Nazism. The alternative type of government advocated by the group was a federal one which stressed morality, individualism and personal freedom.

From the summer of 1942 to February 1943, the White Rose produced six pamphlets, which were distributed by them in the dead of night in Cologne, Innsbruck, Essen, Hannover, Stuttgart, Frankfurt, Nuremberg and Munich. They even distributed leaflets in Linz, where Hitler had spent most of his childhood. Every nocturnal trip by the members of White Rose to deliver their anti-Nazi message carried with it the threat of arrest by the Gestapo. The group also daubed anti-Nazi graffiti on public buildings in many of the major German cities.

All six pamphlets produced by the White Rose stressed that Hitler's regime was evil and corrupt. The first, written in the summer of 1942 by Hans Scholl, urges the German people to sabotage armaments works, boycott meetings of the Nazi Party and generally try to obstruct the war machine of the Nazi regime.[4] The final pamphlet was distributed only a few days after the catastrophic defeat of the German army at the Battle of Stalingrad in February 1943. It is addressed to 'All Germans' and states: 'One can say with mathematical certainty that Hitler is leading Germany over the precipice. Hitler cannot win the war but only extend it. His guilt and that of his aides is beyond measure. His just punishment is coming closer!'[5]

The White Rose pamphlets reveal that public knowledge in Germany of the sorry fate of Jews in the death camps was widespread. One claims that 'since the conquest of Poland 300,000 Jews have been murdered in that country in the most bestial manner' and goes on to point out that Nazi crimes against the Jews were the worst 'in the history of mankind'.[6]

The powerful and well expressed attacks on the Nazi regime in the White Rose pamphlets came to the attention of the Gestapo, which made a determined effort to find out who had produced them. Throughout the winter of 1942–43, the Gestapo started to search for the leading members of the group. The increase in the number of White Rose leaflets circulating in Munich and the presence of anti-Nazi graffiti throughout the city led the Gestapo to conclude that its leaders were operating somewhere in the Munich area and were possibly university lecturers or students. It seems the activities of the White Rose also led to fears on the part of the Nazi authorities that there was a possibility of an anti-Nazi uprising in Bavaria.

In February 1943, Paul Giesler, the Nazi gauleiter (district leader) of Munich, delivered a blunt and uncompromising speech to students at the University of Munich during which he ridiculed male students for being 'physically unfit' to offer service in the German army and advised female students to 'stop wasting their time reading books', find a suitable husband and 'produce a child for the Führer'. Many female students were outraged by the speech and howled down the Nazi gauleiter. Those who had booed Giesler's speech were arrested as they left the hall by members of the Gestapo. There followed a noisy demonstration against Nazi rule, which spread throughout the university campus and then on to the streets of Munich. The student unrest in Munich, which was quickly put down by the Nazi authorities, was the first significant public demonstration against Hitler's rule on the streets of Munich since 1933. The Gestapo decided to place students at the university under strict surveillance.

The end of the White Rose

On 3 February 1943, news of the catastrophic defeat of the German army at the Battle of Stalingrad was announced on German radio. That evening, Sophie and Hans Scholl went out together in the middle of the night and daubed the walls of many university buildings with anti-Nazi slogans. Sophie also wrote the single word 'FREEDOM' near the entrance to the main university lecture hall.

On 4 February 1943, Hans and Sophie Scholl, together with Kurt Huber, produced what turned out to be the final White Rose leaflet, not realising that the Gestapo had the group under close surveillance. The last White Rose leaflet was addressed to 'Fellow Students'. It demanded 'the return of the German nation' from 'the most appalling tyranny that our people has endured'.[7]

Early on the morning of 18 February 1943, Hans and Sophie Scholl decided to distribute the leaflet throughout the university campus. They were carrying a suitcase full of the leaflets through the main university building, dropping leaflets all along the corridor as they walked, when they were suddenly spotted by Jakob Schmidt, the university's head porter, who seized both of them by the arm, shouting, 'You're under arrest'.[8]

The arrest and trial of the members of the White Rose

The Gestapo arrived quickly on campus, having been telephoned by the university's rector. They arrested Hans and Sophie Scholl, who were handcuffed and driven away. Later the same day, Willi Graf was taken into custody, followed the next day by Christoph Probst. Alexander Schmorell was arrested by the Gestapo on 24 February 1943 and Kurt Huber was taken into custody a mere three days later.

Hans and Sophie Scholl were interrogated for over 20 hours at Wittelsbach Palace, the Gestapo headquarters in Munich, before they finally confessed to the authorship of the leaflets. They did not give the names of any of the other members of the White Rose to the Gestapo.

Nazi retribution against Hans and Sophie Scholl was swift and without mercy. A special 'People's Court' was set up, presided over by the notorious Dr Roland Freisler, known as 'Hitler's hanging judge', who was flown in from Berlin specially to deal with members of the White Rose. On Monday 22 February 1943, Sophie Scholl arrived at the court on crutches, with noticeable bruises on her face. Hans Scholl and Christoph Probst showed clear signs that they too had suffered severe physical beatings in the days since their arrest. Hans Scholl tried to make a plea to the court for mercy on behalf of his sister and Christoph Probst (who was married with two children), but Freisler told him to 'shut up' in a very loud voice which boomed around the court room. At the end of the day, Freisler gave the inevitable verdict: all three of the accused were sentenced to die by guillotine immediately.

The leading members of the White Rose accepted the verdict in a calm and dignified manner. They were immediately taken to Stadelheim Prison to await their execution, which was set for 6 p.m. the very same evening. The parents of Hans and Sophie Scholl were allowed a few brief minutes to speak with their children before they were executed. Robert Scholl, with tears in his eyes, warmly embraced his son and daughter, and said to them: 'You will go down in history. There is another justice than this.'[9] Sophie told her father that she was very proud to have stood out against the Nazi regime. By 6.15 p.m. Hans, Sophie and Christoph were all dead. Hans shouted out the single word 'Freedom' before the guillotine fell. Alexander Schmorell and Kurt Huber were both executed on 13 July 1943. Willi Graf, whose trial was delayed, was beheaded on 12 October 1943.

Conclusions

The members of the White Rose carried on their brave and selfless struggle to warn German people of the horrors of Nazi tyranny without any fear of the consequences for their own lives. They had no political agenda, except a deep hatred of Nazism and a yearning for personal freedom. They realised there was unlikely to be any popular backing for their actions.[10] From the very moment the White Rose group gave clear evidence to the Gestapo that they were operating within the University of Munich, their fate was sealed. Nevertheless, the members of the White Rose, although they did not seek immortality, will, as their father told them, 'go down in history' because their morally courageous stand against Hitler's tyranny will shine like a beacon as long as we remember them.

Student protest: the White Rose

3.1 Sophie Scholl on the war – a letter to Fritz Hartnägel, a childhood friend, 9 April 1940

Sometimes this war terrifies me and I could lose all hope. I'd rather not think about it all, but there is hardly anything other than politics, and as long as politics are as muddled and as nasty as now it would be cowardice to turn my back on them. You are probably smiling now, thinking: 'that is a girl talking'. But I believe I would be much more cheerful if I did not have to live with this burden – I could do other things with a clearer conscience. As it is everything has to take second place. Because we had a political upbringing.

Source: 'Letters and notes by Hans and Sophie Scholl', quoted in H. Siefken (ed.), *The White Rose: student resistance to National Socialism 1942–1943*, Nottingham, 1991, p. 200

3.2 Fritz Hartnägel on Sophie Scholl's attitude to the war

It was striking to see with what incisiveness and logic Sophie saw how things would develop, for she was warm hearted and full of feeling, not cold and calculating. Here is an example: in winter 1941–42 there was a big propaganda campaign in Germany to get the people to give sweaters and other warm clothing to the Army . . . Sophie said, 'We're not giving anything'. I had just got back from the Russian Front . . . I tried to describe to her how conditions were for the men, with no gloves, pullovers or warm socks. She stuck to her viewpoint relentlessly and justified it by saying, 'It doesn't matter if it's German soldiers who are freezing to death or Russians, the case is equally terrible. But we must lose the war. If we contribute warm clothes, we'll be extending it.'

Source: A. Gill, *An honourable defeat: a history of German resistance to Hitler*, London, 1994, p. 188

3.3 Hans Scholl dreams of utopia – Hans Scholl's diary, 5 September 1942

A curious idea has driven me to permanent reflection these last few days. I want to create a Utopia . . . I am obsessed with the strange thought that the day might come when war is completely forgotten, because a kind fate has eliminated all memory of it from all books. A true golden age will dawn, such as nobody today could imagine in their wildest dreams. Peace on earth and good will to all men throughout all countries under the sky.

Source: Siefken (ed.), *The White Rose*, p. 214

3.4 Hans Scholl despairs of 'The Germans' – Hans Scholl's diary, 11 September 1942

The Germans are incorrigible. Corruption is so deeply ingrained in them that one cannot remove it without killing the whole body. A lost people. My pessimism increases daily. Scepticism poisons my soul. I want to flee to save it, but where to? In despair, I build a wall around myself made of irony.

Source: Siefken (ed.), *The White Rose*, p. 215

3.5 Sophie Scholl on the 'permanent insecurity' of her life – a letter to Fritz Hartnägel, 7 November 1942

Tonight Hans returns from Russia. I should be glad that he is here with us again . . . And yet I cannot be entirely happy. The permanent insecurity of our life today, which makes it impossible to plan happily for the next day and which casts its shadow over the days which follow, depresses me by day and by night and never really leaves me for a minute . . . Before we speak, we consider every word from all angles to avoid the slightest hint of ambiguity. The trust in other people has to give way to suspicion and caution. Oh, it is tiring and disheartening. But no, nothing shall discourage me, these trivialities will not get the better of me, since I know quite different joys which no one can touch. When I think of that my strength returns and I feel like shouting words of encouragement to all those who are similarly depressed.

Source: Siefken (ed.), *The White Rose*, pp. 215–16

3.6 A White Rose pamphlet, summer 1942

Sabotage armaments-works and war-factories. Sabotage all meetings, assemblies and demonstrations organised by the National Socialist Party. Obstruct the smooth running of the war-machine – a machine that is working for a war whose sole aim is the salvaging and preserving of the National Socialist Party and of its dictatorship. Sabotage all work in the sciences and all intellectual effort which effectively assists the prosecution of the war – in the universities, technical colleges, laboratories, research institutes, technical offices . . .

Source: Siefken (ed.), *The White Rose*, pp. 22–23

Document case-study questions

1 What does 3.1 tell us about Sophie Scholl's attitude towards war?
2 What does 3.2 reveal about Sophie Scholl's views on the German attack on the Soviet Union?
3 What conclusions can be drawn about the attitude of Hans Scholl towards war from 3.3?
4 What does 3.4 tell us about Hans Scholl's attitude towards the German people?
5 How useful is 3.5 for assessing Sophie Scholl's strength of will to oppose the Nazi regime?
6 What conclusions can be drawn about the aims of the White Rose from the evidence in 3.6?

Notes and references

1 For a detailed analysis, see J. P. Stern, 'The White Rose', in H. Siefken (ed.), *The White Rose: student resistance to National Socialism 1942–1943*, Nottingham, 1991, pp. 11–36. See also I. Scholl, *Students against tyranny. The resistance of the White Rose, Munich 1942–1943*, Middletown, CT, 1983.

2 A. Gill, *An honourable defeat: a history of German resistance to Hitler*, London, 1994, p. 187.

3 J. Noakes (ed.), *Nazism 1919–1945, vol. 4: The German home front in World War II*, Exeter, 1998, p. 457.

4 Stern, 'The White Rose', p. 23.

5 Noakes, *Nazism 1919–1945, vol. 4*, p. 457.

6 Stern, 'The White Rose', p. 28.

7 Gill, *An honourable defeat*, p. 192.

8 *Ibid.*, p. 193.

9 *Ibid.*, p. 194.

10 See I. Kershaw, 'Resistance without the people: Bavarian attitudes to the Nazi regime at the time of the White Rose', in Siefken (ed.), *The White Rose*, pp. 51–65.

4 Opposition and resistance from the Christian churches

The Christian churches were the only organisations inside Nazi Germany which professed an alternative belief system to Nazism and were allowed by the regime to retain some semblance of organisational autonomy. Even so, the Nazi regime wanted to force the Christian churches to accept the dominance of Nazi ideology over German society, which required the integration of Nazi ideas into certain aspects of religious practice.

Members of the Christian churches responded to Nazi policy in three different ways. Firstly, many tried to maintain a dual loyalty to Hitler and God in the belief they could support Nazism without betraying their religious principles. Secondly, some Christians concentrated on the narrow objective of maintaining the organisational independence of the churches. Thirdly, a minority of Protestants and Catholics expressed opposition to the attempt of the Nazi regime to undermine long-standing Christian practices and doctrines. The Nazi regime responded to opposition and resistance by arresting and imprisoning some of the leading opponents of its policies within the Christian churches.[1]

The response of the Protestant Church to the Nazi regime

Protestants in Germany during the Nazi era numbered 45 million and belonged to a wide variety of Lutheran and reformed churches, mostly located in north Germany. Article 24 of the political programme of the Nazi Party promised Christians that they could support Nazism without compromising their own religious convictions.

Many Protestant churchgoers, because they were strong supporters of German nationalism, welcomed Hitler's rise to power. Indeed, the hierarchy of the Protestant Church, who were accustomed to working in close co-operation with the state, were initially optimistic about retaining the organisational independence of the Protestant Church within a Nazi state.[2]

The Nazi approach to the Protestant Church

The Nazi regime wanted to create a centralised and unified Protestant Church which would promote Nazi ideology. In July 1933, the 28 provincial Protestant churches were amalgamated to form a single 'Reich Church'. In September 1933, Bishop Ludwig Müller was elected by its synod to be leader of the newly formed body. A second key aim of Nazi policy was to force the Protestant Church to conform to the ideological doctrines of the Nazi Party. Müller, who was Hitler's chief adviser on church affairs, told the Nazi leader that it would be relatively easy to use a fringe Protestant group known as the Faith Movement of German Christians (who were called the 'Nazi stormtroopers of the Church') to force the Protestant Church to follow the doctrines of the Nazi Party. The more extreme members of the German Christians launched a campaign in 1933 (which ended in failure) to have the Old Testament of the Bible removed from Protestant church services on the grounds that it was 'a Jewish book'. Another controversial policy, which Müller pushed through in December 1933, in spite of protests, was the amalgamation of the Evangelical Youth, composed of 700,000 young members of the Protestant Church, into the Hitler Youth.[3] Throughout 1934, Müller also attempted to destroy the independence of the various provincial Protestant and Lutheran churches in Germany.

Conflict between the Nazi state and the principles of Christian faith

The attempt to Nazify Protestantism in Germany provoked a strong reaction within the Protestant Church, which aimed to defend traditional values and church institutions. This drive to resist Nazi control was boosted by widespread grass-roots support from Protestant churchgoers.

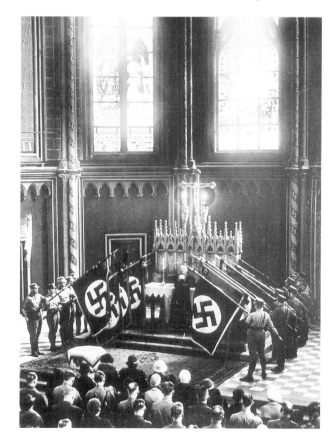

Nazis blatantly displaying Swastika flags at a memorial service for an SA officer in a Berlin church in 1934.

31

A more radical form of resistance to the Nazi regime was offered by a minority group within the Protestant Church called the 'Confessing Church', established in September 1933 by the Reverend Martin Niemöller, who rejected the Nazi claim to authority over the practices of Christianity within the Protestant Church. Niemöller persuasively argued that the primary allegiance of the Protestant clergy was to God, not Nazi ideology. The members of the Confessing Church, who viewed themselves as the 'true custodians of the Protestant faith', mounted a brave campaign of opposition to the attempts of the German Christians to Nazify the church.[4] Indeed, in May 1936 the Church leaders sent a memorandum to Hitler denouncing the 'de-Christianising of German life' by the Nazi regime.

The Nazi regime responded to the resistance activities of the Confessing Church by placing its supporters under surveillance. In many cases, pastors were removed from their parishes by the Gestapo and incarcerated in concentration camps. In July 1937, Niemöller was placed in 'protective custody', in a concentration camp, where he was to remain until his release in 1945. In addition, in March of that year, 800 pastors who supported the Confessing Church had also been detained in concentration camps.

The 'church struggle' proved very embarrassing for the Nazi regime. In 1937, Hitler tried to take the heat out of the 'church struggle' by returning control of the Protestant Church to the official Church establishment in return for a promise that it would maintain loyalty towards the state. As a result, the attempt to Nazify the Protestant Church was abandoned and the influence of the German Christians went into steep decline. The struggle by the Protestant Church to defend its religious and organisational independence was strengthened by the support of millions of Protestant churchgoers.

The limits of Protestant resistance

However, opposition to Nazi attacks on the Church did not imply disapproval by the Protestant Church of Hitler's foreign policy or the expansion of German armaments. There was also hardly any opposition expressed among the Protestant clergy to the persecution of the Jews in Germany. Even the Confessing Church stressed it was defending the principle of non-interference by the state in religious practices – not trying to oppose the domestic or foreign policies of the regime or advocating its overthrow. Indeed, Martin Niemöller, who had been a member of the National Conservative Party and who had served as a U-boat captain in the First World War, greeted Hitler's rise to power in 1933 with enthusiasm. Niemöller even offered to fight for Germany during the Second World War.

It is probably worth adding that the only leading Protestant pastor involved in the active German resistance was Dietrich Bonhoeffer, who helped to build up overseas contacts for the resistance. Bonhoeffer joined the Confessing Church in 1935. He was critical of the Nazi regime and by 1940 had been banned from preaching and publishing on church affairs. In 1943, he was arrested by the Gestapo and was executed in Flossenbürg concentration camp in April 1945.

Dietrich Bonhoeffer (1906–45) in the courtyard of his Berlin prison in 1944.

The Catholic Church and the Nazi regime

The Catholic Church was more united in outlook than the Protestant Church. The allegiance of German Catholics, based mostly in south Germany, to Roman Catholicism had survived the Reformation. Before 1933, the majority of Catholic voters were hostile to the Nazi Party and remained loyal to the Catholic Centre Party. In March 1933, the Catholic Centre Party supported the passing of the Enabling Act, but most Catholics remained quite sceptical about the Nazi regime.[5]

The Concordat between the Catholic Church and the Nazi regime

In July 1933, Hitler (who had been baptised a Catholic) signed a 'Concordat' with the Vatican, the centre of the Catholic Church, based in Rome. Under the terms of the Concordat, Hitler promised to guarantee the Catholic Church the right to regulate its own affairs, provided it voluntarily disbanded the Catholic Centre Party and withdrew from politics. Most Catholic bishops viewed the Concordat as a guarantee of non-interference by the Nazis in the affairs of the Catholic Church.[6]

However, the Nazi regime frequently violated the terms of the Concordat by suppressing the religious activities of Catholic schools, by banning Catholic youth organisations and by closing down Catholic newspapers. The regime also mounted a press campaign of vilification against Catholic priests and nuns, which accused them of engaging in 'immoral sexual activities'.

Protest by Catholics against the Nazi regime

These developments led to the growth of opposition from Catholics to the Nazi regime. Yet opposition to Nazi church policy was not led by the Catholic Church's hierarchy, which at no time questioned the legality of the Nazi regime, but rather by Catholic priests, supported by local parish members. At the grass-roots level, priests organised opposition to the banning of Catholic youth organisations, the closing down of Catholic schools and the gagging of the Catholic press. Many Catholic churchgoers displayed loyalty to the Church by participating in pilgrimages to holy sites.

During 1936, the Catholic Church fought a successful battle with the Nazi regime to retain the use of the crucifix in churches. In March 1937, Pope Pius XI gave a speech entitled 'With Burning Concern' (the text of which was circulated by Catholic priests throughout Germany), which contained criticism of Nazi policies towards the Catholic Church in Germany and urged Adolf Hitler to adhere to the principles laid down in the Concordat. A few Catholic bishops, most notably Clemens Graf von Galen, spoke out in 1941 against the systematic murder of the mentally ill undertaken by the Nazi regime through its controversial euthanasia programme (codenamed the T4 programme). Many other Catholic bishops spoke out in opposition to the sterilisation policies of the regime. Most Catholics, unlike committed Nazis, placed too much value on

Bishop Graf von Galen
(1878–1946).

individual human life ever to accept the central Nazi idea of a socially engineered 'master race'.

The strength of Catholic participation in resistance activities directed against the Nazi regime is emphasised by the fact that 400 Catholic priests were incarcerated in the Dachau concentration camp alone. Indeed, the majority of Gestapo reports on religious opponents of the Nazi regime related to members of the Catholic Church. Catholic opposition towards the regime was boosted by the large growth in attendance at Catholic churches. By and large, the Nazi regime regarded the Catholic Church as a formidable opponent which opposed Nazi biological and racist eugenic ideology and attempted, with great vigour and some success, to defend its institutional and spiritual independence. It is, perhaps, no coincidence that Stauffenberg, who attempted the assassination of Hitler on 20 July 1944, was a Catholic.

Conclusions

There is no doubt that the attempt by the Nazi regime to undermine the traditional religious practices of the Christian churches was met by a determination to uphold the independence of the churches from Nazi domination. What the Christian churches defended was their right to oppose the Nazi drive to impose its will over every aspect of German life. As a result, the churches were challenging the totalitarian claims of the Nazi dictatorship but not publicly endorsing it.

Document case study

Opposition and resistance from the Christian churches

4.1 Hitler outlines Nazi policy towards the churches, March 1933

The national government regards the two Christian confessions as the most important factors for the preservation of our national culture. It will honour the treaties between them and the provincial government. Their rights will not be infringed. It does, however, hope and trust that the work for the national and moral renewal of our nation, which the government has taken upon it, will for its part be given like approval . . . The national government will guarantee the Christian confessions their due influence in school and educational matters. It is concerned to foster a frank and harmonious relationship between church and state. The fight against a materialistic view of the world and for the creation of a genuine national community is as much in the interests of the German nation as those of our Christian faith. Likewise the government of the Reich, which regards Christianity as the unshakable foundation of our national life and morality, regards the fostering and the extension of the friendly relations to the Holy See [i.e. the Vatican] as a matter of the greatest importance. The rights of the churches will not be restricted, nor will their relationship to the state be changed.

Source: P. Matheson (ed.), *The Third Reich and the Christian churches*, Edinburgh, 1981, p. 9

4.2 The aims of the German Christians, May 1933

The national uprising in our fatherland has enabled the German state and the German people to find their way to one another's hearts in a quite new way. It seems now that the German people, reflecting on the deepest sources of its life and energy, wishes also to find its way back to the church. For a German church merely co-existing with the German people is nothing but an empty institution. It will only be a Christian church in the midst of the German people when it is a church on behalf of the German people, helping the German people in selfless service to recognise and carry out its God-given calling . . . As a result the tasks confronting the church as well as the state have grown stupendously. In their present form the German churches are incapable of carrying out these tasks. The aim of the 'German Christians' is to provide the German churches with a forum which will enable them to serve the German people in the specific ways the Gospel of Jesus Christ lays upon them for the service of their own people . . . We want through our Church to serve our God, and thereby our fatherland.

Source: Matheson (ed.), *The Third Reich and the Christian churches*, p. 9

4.3 The major terms of the Concordat between the Vatican and the Third Reich, July 1933

Article 1
The German Reich guarantees freedom of belief and of public worship to the Catholic faith. It recognises the right of the Catholic Church – within the limits of the law of the land – to order and administer its own affairs and to make laws and regulations binding upon its members in matters within its competence . . .
Article 5
The clergy enjoys the protection of the state in the exercise of their spiritual office in the same way as state officials. The state will prosecute insults to their persons . . .
Article 9
Clergy cannot be questioned by judicial and other authorities about facts confided to them in the exercise of their spiritual guidance and which therefore come under the obligation to pastoral confidentiality . . .
Article 14
1. Catholic clergy who hold ecclesiastical office in Germany or exercise pastoral functions or educational functions, must (a) be German citizens, (b) have the qualification to study at a German institute of higher education, (c) have studied theology and philosophy for at least three years in a German university, a German ecclesiastical academy, or a papal college in Rome.
Article 15
Monastic orders and religious associations . . . are not subject to any special restrictions by the state.
Article 16
Before bishops enter upon the government of their dioceses they are to take an oath of fealty to the representative of the Reich government in the provinces or to the president of the Reich in the following words: 'Before God and on the Holy Gospel I swear and promise – as becomes a bishop – loyalty to the German Reich and to the state.' . . .

Article 19

The Catholic theological faculties in the universities will remain in being . . .

Article 21

Instruction in the Catholic faith is a regular part of the curriculum in the elementary, technical, intermediate, and high schools and is taught in accordance with the principles of the Catholic Church . . . The syllabus and the selection of text-books for religious instruction will be determined with the agreement of the church authorities . . .

Article 23

The retention and establishment of Catholic confessional schools is guaranteed . . .

Article 27

Special pastoral provision will be made for the Catholic officers, officials and men of the German army, together with their families . . .

Article 31

The property and activities of those Catholic organisations and associations whose aims are purely religious, cultural or charitable and which, therefore, are under the authority of the hierarchy, will be protected . . .

Article 33

Should differences of opinion arise in future as to the interpretation or application of any of the terms of the concordat the Holy See and the German Reich will consult together to resolve the matter in a friendly manner.

Source: Matheson (ed.), *The Third Reich and the Christian churches*, pp. 29–33

4.4 Report of a meeting between Hitler and Protestant Church leaders, January 1934

Niemöller . . . stressed that his struggle was not directed against the Third Reich, but that it . . . was for the sake of this Reich. Hitler countered very sharply that concern for the Third Reich should be left to him . . . In a passionate tone the Chancellor [Hitler] complained that this conflict in the evangelical church, because of its exploitation by the foreign press, made the position of the Third Reich much more difficult . . . He had tried to help the church forward, as it had to a large degree lost touch with the masses of the people . . . He had not forced Müller [the Reich Bishop] upon us, but we could not drop him after only four months, but should make another real attempt to co-operate with him. He himself [Hitler] had been born a Catholic. He was thankful to destiny for this, since it enabled him to win millions of Catholics too, to National Socialism . . . The church leaders of our group emphasised that isolated expressions of political discontent could not be urged as evidence of reactionary sentiments among the pastorate as a whole . . . The Reich Chancellor concluded with an urgent appeal to join forces in a Christian and brotherly way with the Reich Bishop and so end the conflict which, because of the political situation, could no longer be tolerated.

Source: Matheson (ed.), *The Third Reich and the Christian churches*, pp. 42–44

4.5 SS report on the activities of Catholic priests, June 1934

The most dangerous activity of countless Catholic clergy is the way in which they 'mope about', spreading despondence. Favourite topics are the 'dangers of a new time', 'the present emergency', 'the gloomy future'. Prophesies are made about the speedy downfall of National Socialism or at the very least mention is made of the transience of all political phenomena, compared with the Catholic Church which will outlive them all. National Socialist achievements and successes are passed over in silence. There is thus a deliberate undermining of the very basis of the National Socialist programme of reconstruction, the people's trust in the leadership of the state.

Source: Matheson (ed.), *The Third Reich and the Christian churches*, pp. 48–49

4.6 'With Burning Concern' – an open letter by Pope Pius XI, March 1937

With burning concern and mounting consternation we have been observing for some time now the cross carried by the church in Germany and the increasingly difficult situation of those men and women who have kept faith and remained true to her in thought and deed . . . When we, reverend brethren, accepted the proposal of the Reich government in the summer of 1933 to engage in negotiations about a concordat on the basis of a draft dating back several years, these negotiations ended, to the satisfaction of all of you, with solemn agreement . . . Anyone who has within him the slightest feelings for truth, whose heart has even a shadowy sense of justice will have to admit then that in these difficult and eventful years which have followed the Concordat every one of our words and our deeds have been regulated by loyalty to the agreement that was made. He will, however, also have to note with consternation and deepest disapproval how for the other side it has become the unwritten law of their conduct [the Nazi regime's] to misconstrue, evade, undermine, and in the end more or less openly violate the treaty.

Source: Matheson (ed.), *The Third Reich and the Christian churches*, pp. 67–71

4.7 Church opposition – a poem by Martin Niemöller, leader of the Confessing Church

When the Nazis came for the Communists
I was silent
I wasn't a Communist
When the Nazis came for the Social Democrats
I was silent
I wasn't a Social Democrat
When the Nazis came for the Trade Unionists
I was silent
I wasn't a Trade Unionist
When the Nazis came for the Jews
I was silent
I wasn't a Jew
When the Nazis came for me
There was no one left
To Protest

Source: A. Gill, *An honourable defeat: a history of German resistance to Hitler*, London, 1994, p. 63

Document case-study questions

1 What does 4.1 suggest about Hitler's policy towards the Christian churches?
2 What does 4.2 tell us about the attitude of the German Christians towards Christian belief?
3 What rights does 4.3 give to Catholics in Nazi Germany?
4 What impression does 4.4 give of Hitler's views on the Confessing Church?
5 What is the attitude of the SS officer in 4.5 towards Catholic priests?
6 Assess the usefulness of 4.6 for a historian attempting to evaluate whether the Concordat was being adhered to by the Nazi regime.
7 What does 4.7 reveal about Niemöller's attitude towards the Nazi regime?

Notes and references

1 For a detailed examination of the Christian churches under the Nazi regime, see E. Helmrich, *The German churches under Hitler*, Detroit, 1979.
2 See H. Graml, H. Mommsen, H-J. Reichhardt and E. Wolf, *The German resistance to Hitler*, London, 1970, pp. 199–229.
3 P. Matheson (ed.), *The Third Reich and the Christian churches*, Edinburgh, 1981, pp. 40–41.
4 For a detailed discussion of resistance activities by Protestants, see R. Ericksen, 'A radical minority: resistance in the German Protestant Church', in F. Nicosia and L. Stokes (eds.), *Germans against Nazism: nonconformity, opposition and resistance in the Third Reich*, Oxford, 1990, pp. 115–36.
5 For a detailed examination of resistance to Nazism from the Catholic Church, see D. Dietrich, 'Catholic resistance to biological and racist eugenics in the Third Reich', in Nicosia and Stokes, *Germans against Nazism*, pp. 137–56.
6 For a full text of the terms of the Concordat, see Matheson, *The Third Reich and the Christian churches*, pp. 29–33.

The conservative and military resistance against Hitler

In the early years of the Third Reich, Hitler ruled through an alliance between old conservative groups and a new Nazi elite. Towards the end of the 1930s, however, many members of the old conservative elites felt that the power balance within Germany was shifting markedly towards the Nazis. One of the major concerns of the conservative old guard was that Hitler's aggressive foreign policy would plunge Germany into a European war it would eventually lose. In addition, many conservatives were concerned about the growing brutality of the Nazi regime and shocked by the persecution of the Christian churches. As a consequence, conservative and military leaders drew together to form secretive resistance groups united in a determination to overthrow Hitler's regime.

The Beck–Goerdeler group

The leading conservative and military resistance faction, led by General Ludwig Beck and Carl Goerdeler, was known as the Beck–Goerdeler group. This group was behind the 1944 bomb plot on Hitler's life, discussed in Chapter 6. Beck was chief of the army general staff from 1935 to 1938. He welcomed Hitler's 'national revolution' in 1933 because it promised to destroy Communism and build up the strength of the army. However, Beck became progressively alarmed about the implications for European peace of Hitler's aggressive foreign policy. During 1938, he became especially worried by Hitler's determination to engineer a European war over the seemingly minor issue of a group of 3.5 million German-speakers in the Sudeten region of Czechoslovakia being incorporated into Germany.

To prevent Germany being plunged into an unnecessary war, Beck decided to mount a coup by a small group of army officers to overthrow Hitler's regime. To this end, he sent a few officers to Britain in order to warn of Hitler's burning desire to 'crush Czechoslovakia' by military force. However, Beck's conspiracy came to nothing for two important reasons. Firstly, Colonel General Walther von Brauchitsch, the German military commander in chief, supported by most of the leading German generals, refused to support the conspiracy (though their loyalty to the army officer class meant that they did not betray it). Secondly, Neville Chamberlain, the British Prime Minister, who was enthusiastically following a policy of appeasement towards Nazi Germany, refused to give any encouragement to the plan. Utterly dismayed, Beck resigned as chief of the army general staff in August 1938, but soon emerged as the leading military figure in a

General Ludwig Beck (1880–1944).

complex network of conspirators who aimed to bring about the fall of the Nazi regime.

The second key figure in the conservative resistance against Hitler was Carl Friedrich Goerdeler, a German nationalist who was the mayor of Leipzig from 1930 to 1937.[1] In November 1934, he was appointed Reich Commissioner for Price Control in Hitler's government. However, Goerdeler became increasingly disillusioned by the Nazi regime during the late 1930s. He resigned from the Nazi government in 1935. He also gave up the post of mayor of Leipzig in 1937 in protest over the removal from Leipzig town centre of a statue of Felix Mendelssohn, the Jewish composer. From 1937 onwards, Goerdeler became the leading civilian figure in the conservative–military resistance against the Nazi regime, building an impressive network of supporters inside Nazi Germany and developing useful diplomatic contacts abroad.[2]

Because Hitler's troops were marching from victory to victory in the early battles of the Second World War, resistance leaders had very little opportunity of winning support within the army – or among the German people – for the overthrow of the Nazi dictator. However, by 1941, Goerdeler had been able to establish a small informal group of sympathisers (known as the Beck–Goerdeler group), who discussed the idea of overthrowing Hitler's regime. The group co-ordinated the conservative–military resistance against Hitler, engaged in discussions with like-minded people, established important diplomatic contacts abroad and worked on detailed plans to bring about the fall of Hitler.

The Beck–Goerdeler group contained two different elements: an older generation of German conservative nationalists, diplomats and generals; and a

Carl Friedrich Goerdeler
(1884–1945).

younger generation of diplomats and army officers. The older group looked back nostalgically to Germany before 1914 and most of them were opposed to democracy. Beck, for example, believed the German army should have continued to fight in the First World War in order to save the German monarch. However, many of the younger members of the group were much less attracted to the idea of turning the clock back towards the era of the kaiser and desired a post-Hitler Germany to be based on more democratic principles.[3]

The importance of the army

The Beck–Goerdeler group realised that the German army was best placed to strike a decisive blow against Hitler's regime. As a result, the group made strenuous efforts to win support among Hitler's military commanders. In March 1943, Goerdeler sent a memorandum to generals urging a coup. The leading army officers who supported the Beck–Goerdeler group were Henning von Tresckow, a key figure in command of army group centre on the eastern front; Field Marshal Erwin von Witzleben, who had retired but had previously occupied several positions in the German high command; and Claus von Stauffenberg, a colonel in the German army. The Beck–Goerdeler group also tried to gain the support of Field Marshal Günther von Kluge, the commander of army group centre, but he refused to join the conspiracy. The number of army officers in the Beck–Goerdeler group increased as the fortunes of the German army plummeted in the war against the Soviet Union after its defeat at Stalingrad in February 1943.

The plans for government of the Beck–Goerdeler group

It is important to examine the plans for government and the policy ideas of the Beck–Goerdeler group in order to establish why they opposed Hitler and what type of regime they wanted in place of Nazism. They wanted to create a government based on the rule of law, with free speech, religious freedom and social justice. However, they did not want post-Hitler Germany to have a parliamentary system with competing political parties. On the contrary, they wanted to create a state with a dominant leader, supported by a hand-picked elite, who controlled parliament, but with a system of local government which allowed maximum freedom for local people to make local decisions. Goerdeler was designated as Chancellor and Beck was to be head of state (whom the conspirators dubbed the 'Regent').

In foreign policy, the most important aim of the Beck–Goerdeler group was to negotiate a peace settlement with the western Allies, which they hoped would lay the basis for peaceful co-operation in Europe. The exact role the 'new Germany' should play in post-war Europe was a matter of debate within the group. Some of the older members wanted Germany to remain a major military and economic power, while the younger members believed that Germany should support the formation of a union of European nations (similar to the modern-day European Union). On the Jewish question, they proposed the creation of an independent Jewish state.

To the British and American diplomatic officials who held secret talks with representatives of the Beck–Goerdeler group during 1941 to 1944, the foreign policy objectives of the group appeared extremely militaristic. They seemed to want Britain and America to abandon the wartime alliance with the Soviet Union and enter a pact with figures within an army which the Allies were united against. Indeed, it seemed to these diplomats that the Beck–Goerdeler group wanted the achievement of many of Hitler's foreign policy aims by more peaceful means.[4]

Opponents in the Foreign Office

Very closely linked to the Beck–Goerdeler group were opponents of the Nazi regime within the Foreign Office, a body which had never become a fully fledged Nazi organisation. Members of the old upper-class elite who occupied the main positions in the German Foreign Office were not committed Nazis and became deeply concerned during the late 1930s that Hitler's aggressive foreign policy would produce a world war, which Germany would ultimately lose. As a result, a number of Foreign Office diplomats worked closely with the Beck–Goerdeler group to build up overseas diplomatic contacts.

The two leading members of the Beck–Goerdeler group in the Foreign Office were: Adam von Trott zu Solz, who engaged in detailed diplomatic negotiations with British and American officials in Switzerland and Sweden, with the aim of finding a possible diplomatic agreement with Britain and America; and Ulrich von Hassell, a former German ambassador in Rome, who believed that Germany was heading for inevitable military defeat. Hassell engaged in clandestine diplomatic negotiations on behalf of the conservative–military resistance with British intelligence and diplomatic sources, in the hope of negotiating a peace settlement.[5]

Abwehr

Another group closely linked with the Beck–Goerdeler group was Abwehr, the military intelligence wing of the German Foreign Office. The members of Abwehr supplied vital information concerning Hitler's movements and military plans to the leaders of the Beck–Goerdeler group. Abwehr was also a very useful means of passing information between the Beck–Goerdeler group and diplomatic officials in Britain and America. Abwehr also put together a secret dossier which detailed Nazi war crimes in the occupied territories (known as the Zossen documents). These documents were to be used in a proposed trial of leading Nazis for war crimes.

The two leading figures in Abwehr were: Admiral Wilhelm Canaris, an ardent monarchist, who believed Hitler's regime had to be toppled from within (he resigned, under pressure from the Gestapo, in February 1944 and was arrested after the bomb plot of July 1944); and Major General Hans Oster, chief of the Central Department, who drew together the plans of the army group of conspirators. Oster, who, surprisingly for a spy, was unable to keep a secret, was arrested by the Gestapo in early 1944.[6] Both men were executed in April 1945.

The Kreisau Circle

There were other conservative groups who discussed what type of political order should be established after the fall of Hitler's regime. The most significant of these fringe groups was the Kreisau Circle, which took its name from the country estate of its leader, Helmuth James von Moltke, the great-grandnephew of a famous Prussian field marshal.

The members of the Kreisau Circle came from diverse backgrounds and included Protestant and Catholic churchgoers, aristocrats, Foreign Office officials and one or two left-wing figures. The group met sporadically between 1942 and 1944 at Kreisau Castle and in the apartments of sympathisers in the affluent Berlin suburbs.

The Kreisau Circle wanted to restore personal freedom and the rule of law throughout Germany, and replace the cult of the leader and the party with a democratic system in which self-governing regions would govern for the benefit of local communities. They also advocated the creation of a federal Europe (similar to the European Union) in order to end European conflict. The democratic ideas of the Kreisau Circle did not meet with the general approval of most of the leading conservative figures in the Beck–Goerdeler group, but they did prove attractive to many of the younger officers involved in the conspiracy to kill Hitler, especially to Stauffenberg, who believed only a broad-based coalition involving individuals from the labour movement as well as Liberals and Social Democrats could hope to win support from the German people.

The Gestapo discovered the Kreisau Circle during the winter of 1943–44. In January 1944, Moltke was arrested and subsequently executed. In spite of Moltke's arrest, the Kreisau Circle continued to meet. Peter Graf Yorck von Wartenburg, who was the cousin of Stauffenberg, assumed leadership of the group after Moltke's arrest. In discussions with Stauffenberg, the Kreisau Circle agreed to accept Carl Goerdeler as the leader of the 'transitional government' which was designated to replace Hitler. It has also recently been shown that Yorck became a close adviser to Stauffenberg on administrative and social reform before the attempt on Hitler's life in July 1944. Indeed, the Kreisau Circle, often depicted by some historians as a group of 'idealists', with no real link to the conspiracy to overthrow Hitler, represented a very important policy think-tank which had close contact with younger members of the army conspiracy. If Stauffenberg had killed Hitler, then the leaders of the Kreisau Circle would have been a key part of a post-Hitler government.[7]

The conservative and military resistance against Hitler

5.1 The foreign policy aims of the Beck–Goerdeler group – a secret memorandum, 1941

All Germans who live together belong in a nation-state; it does not weaken Germany's prestige if substantial numbers of Germans live outside of the German Reich . . . Germany's central position in a group of other nation-states compels the German Reich to maintain a sufficiently strong Army. This must also be secured on the diplomatic front. Whether it will provide the core of European military forces depends on future developments . . . The maintenance of the German Army is so important that this factor should be placed at the forefront when considering the timing and the form of the conclusion of peace. The Army is also essential as a domestic political bond and as a school for the nation . . . The development of technology requires larger economic spheres than those created during the nineteenth century . . . The greater economic area which is appropriate for Germany is certainly Europe . . . If it is to have any hope of lasting, the European economic sphere can only be achieved through the organic union of independent European nation-states and not by forcing them together . . . Its central position, its demographic strength and its high level of capability will guarantee the German people leadership of the European bloc if it does not destroy its chance through lack of moderation or through a bullying manner. It is stupid and arrogant to talk of Germans as a master race. It is foolish to demand respect for one's own national honour and independence and to deny them to others. The nation which respects the small nations and which tries to guide their fortunes with wise counsel and a wise hand and not with brutal force will grow into the leadership of Europe . . . The union of

45

Europe must not occur crudely and ruthlessly through coordination but can only happen if it is based on the wisdom which Bismarck embodied in the case of the unification of Germany . . . In the east a fruitful economic and political cooperation cannot develop with a Bolshevik Russia . . . It is advisable in all circumstances to maintain permanent contact with England, the USA, China and Japan . . . It is useful for the German Reich to possess colonies . . . A concentrated block of colonial territory is generally preferable to one that is scattered far and wide . . . Any discussion of disarmament can and must be initially rejected. But the exhaustion of economic resources compels every major state to make cuts and in the end to seek agreement on a sensible degree of disarmament . . . A rearrangement of the position of the Jews appears necessary throughout the world . . . The fact that the Jewish people belong to another race is a commonplace. Among the Jewish people there is disagreement as to whether they should seek to form an independent state or not. The Zionists have been demanding and preparing for their own Jewish state for a long time. Up until 1933 they did not play an important role. However, the world will only find peace if the Jewish people acquire a really effective opportunity to found and maintain their own state.

Source: J. Noakes (ed.), *Nazism 1919–1945: a documentary reader, vol. 4: The German home front in World War II*, Exeter, 1998, pp. 600–03

5.2 The reactionary nature of the Beck–Goerdeler group – the concerns of Ulrich von Hassell, secret memorandum, 1941

What has engrossed and disquieted me most during the past weeks has been the numerous conferences on questions concerning a change of regime. One major difficulty is Goerdeler. He is too sanguine, always sees things as he wishes to see them, and in many ways is a real reactionary . . . The principal difficulty with Beck is that he is very theoretical . . . a man of tactics, but little will power . . . I have always feared that we have too little contact with younger circles . . . First of all I had a long talk with Trott [Adam von Trott zu Solz], during which he passionately contended for the avoidance, within as well as outside the country, of any semblance of 'reaction', of a 'gentleman's club', or of 'militarism'. Therefore, though he is also a monarchist, we must under no circumstances have a monarchy, for a monarchy would not win the support of the people or win confidence abroad . . . To these negative points he added the single positive thought, that Niemoeller should be made Chancellor. He was, on the one hand, the strongest internationally recognized exponent of anti-Hitlerism, and, on the other hand, the most popular reformer here and the most likely to appeal to the Anglo-Saxon world. Afterwards I met the alert, cultured Peter Yorck [a leading figure in the Kreisau Circle] . . . He expressed similar sentiments . . . Goerdeler takes an almost completely unsympathetic attitude towards the ideas of these young men, who for their part disapprove of him . . . Goerdeler, of course, overestimates the degree to which people in general resent the present system and long for a move towards liberation.

Source: U. von Hassell, *The von Hassell diaries 1938–1945*, London, 1948, pp. 209–11

5.3 Goerdeler appeals to the army high command to join the resistance against Hitler – a letter from Goerdeler to Field Marshal Günther von Kluge, commander of army group centre, July 1943

In view of the national disaster which is evidently developing and into which we have been plunged by a crazed leadership, which despises all divine and human law, I am taking the liberty of addressing a final request to you, Herr Field Marshal. You may be certain that it will be the last. The time has now come for us to reach a final decision on our personal fates. The path to which our consciences direct us leads in one direction; the other, the easier one points in the other direction. The one involves dangers but is honourable; the other will lead to the bitter end and fearful remorse . . . It is obvious that no statesman in the world will be prepared to negotiate with criminals . . . I have once more established and take responsibility for saying that there is still a possibility of securing a favourable peace for us if we Germans once more transform ourselves into a people with whom it is feasible to negotiate . . . We must stop permitting fools to impose their illusions and lies on the German people . . .

Source: Noakes (ed.), *Nazism 1919–1945, vol. 4*, pp. 610–11

5.4 Basic principles of a new order in Germany – a secret memorandum of the Kreisau Circle, August 1943

The Government of the German Reich sees in Christianity the basis for the moral and religious revival of our people, for the overcoming of hatred and lies, for the reconstruction of the European community of nations.

1. Justice which has been trampled underfoot must be raised again and made predominant over all areas of life . . .

2. Freedom of faith and of conscience will be safeguarded. Existing laws and regulations which violate these principles will be repealed at once . . .

3. Totalitarian moral restraint must be broken and the inviolable dignity of the human person must be recognised as the basis for the order of justice and peace which is to be striven for . . .

4. The basic unit of peaceful social life is the family . . .

5. Work must be organised in such a way that it promotes personal responsibility and does not let it wither . . .

6. The political responsibility of every individual demands his cooperation in the self-government which is to be revived . . .

7. The special responsibility and loyalty due from every individual to his national origin, to his language and to the intellectual and historical traditions of his people must be safeguarded and respected . . .

The Reich will be structured on the principle of self-administration. It will combine freedom and personal responsibility with the requirements of order and leadership . . . The Reich parliament will be elected by the provincial parliaments. Every male Reich citizen who has reached the age of 27 is entitled to be elected [females were excluded].

Source: Noakes (ed.), *Nazism 1919–1945, vol. 4*, pp. 614–16

5.5 The views of a leading member of the Kreisau Circle on the dangers of mounting opposition to the Nazi regime – a letter from Helmuth von Moltke to Lionel Curtis, a friend in England, 1942

We can only expect to get our people to overthrow this reign of terror and horror if we are able to show a picture beyond the terrifying and hopeless immediate future. A picture which will make it worth while for the disillusioned people to strive for, to work for, to start again and to believe in. For us Europe after the war is a question of how the picture of man can be re-established in the breasts of our fellow citizens. This is a question of religion and education, of ties to work and family, of the proper relation of responsibilities and rights. I must say that under the incredible burden under which we have to labour we have made progress, which will be visible one day. Can you imagine what it means to work as a group when you cannot use the telephone, when you are unable to post letters, when you cannot tell the names of your closest friends to your other friends for fear one of them might be caught and might divulge the names under pressure? . . . We hope that you will realise that we are ready to help you win the war and peace.

Source: Noakes (ed.), *Nazism 1919–1945, vol. 4*, pp. 610–11

Document case-study questions

1 Offer an evaluation of the foreign policy aims of the Beck–Goerdeler group, outlined in 5.1.

2 Identify three major criticisms which Hassell makes about Carl Goerdeler in 5.2.

3 What points does Goerdeler emphasise in 5.3 in order to win over Kluge to the resistance struggle?

4 How would you describe the type of government which is outlined by the Kreisau Circle in 5.4?

5 What insights does 5.5 provide concerning the difficulties of engaging in resistance against the Nazi regime?

Notes and references

1 G. Ritter, *The German resistance: Carl Goerdeler's struggle against tyranny*, London, 1958.

2 See K-J. Müller, 'The structure and nature of the national conservative opposition in Germany up to 1940', in H. Köch (ed.), *Aspects of the Third Reich*, New York, 1985.

3 See L. Hill, 'The national–conservatives and opposition to the Third Reich before the Second World War', in F. Nicosia and L. Stokes (eds.), *Germans against Nazism: nonconformity, opposition and resistance in the Third Reich*, Oxford, 1990, pp. 221–52.

4 See P. Steinbach, 'The Conservative resistance', in D. Large (ed.), *Contending with Hitler*, Cambridge, 1991, pp. 89–98.

5 K. von Klemperer, *German resistance against Hitler*, Oxford, 1992, pp. 25–36.

6 *Ibid.*, pp. 23–25.

7 See T. Childers, 'The Kreisau Circle and the twentieth of July', in Large (ed.), *Contending with Hitler*, pp. 99–118.

20 July 1944: Stauffenberg and the bomb attempt on Hitler's life

The resistance against Hitler from within conservative and military circles culminated in the failed assassination attempt on Hitler's life by Claus von Stauffenberg, which took place on 20 July 1944, when a bomb exploded during a meeting Hitler was attending at his military headquarters at Rastenburg, in east Prussia. Hitler survived with only very minor injuries. In the aftermath of the plot, the conservative–military resistance which had been built up over many years was ferociously destroyed in a brutal Nazi blood purge.

Claus von Stauffenberg

Colonel Claus Graf Schenck von Stauffenberg was the person who attempted to kill Adolf Hitler.[1] He was born in Jettingen, into a wealthy south German aristocratic family, in 1907. His family was steeped in military tradition. Stauffenberg was the great-grandson of a Prussian military hero from the Napoleonic Wars. During the 1930s he rose effortlessly up the ranks of the German army.

Claus von Stauffenberg (1907–44).

It was during the German campaign against the Soviet Union, which began in June 1941, that Stauffenberg became disillusioned with Hitler's rule. In August 1942, he told a friend: 'They are shooting Jews in masses. These crimes must not be allowed to continue.'[2] After that summer, he was convinced that Hitler had to be overthrown, and to achieve this objective he became closely involved in the plans and schemes of the Beck–Goerdeler group.

In 1943, Stauffenberg was sent to Tunisia in order to help in the fruitless German attempt to halt the rapid advance of the western Allies in North Africa. He had been transferred to North Africa on the orders of General Kurt Zeitzler, a leading German general, loyal to Hitler, who had tolerated Stauffenberg's anti-Hitler views for some time, but came to the conclusion that it might be a good idea to post the headstrong officer away from the main theatre of war in Europe. Stauffenberg agreed to go because he was disappointed with the lack of response from the German officer class to his idea of assassinating Hitler.

On 7 April 1943, Stauffenberg's car was hit by heavy machine gun fire from an American warplane. He lost an eye, his right hand and two fingers of his left hand in the incident. These injuries seem to have made him even more disillusioned with Hitler's regime. Because of his serious injuries, Stauffenberg could easily have opted to retire from the army on health grounds, but he chose not to, for one single purpose: to kill Adolf Hitler.

Planning to kill Hitler

On his return to Germany, Stauffenberg learned, as he recovered from his injuries, that Beck had given the go-ahead for the assassination of Hitler. Goerdeler supported the plot to overthrow the regime by force, but he opposed killing Hitler, preferring instead to put him on trial for his war crimes.

During 1943, there were six separate attempts by members of the army resistance to assassinate the Nazi dictator. The army plotters nearly succeeded on 13 March 1943 when a time bomb smuggled on to Hitler's airplane (on a flight from Smolensk to his military headquarters at Rastenburg) failed to explode. One of the major problems facing the army resistance was Hitler's own strong fear of assassination, which encouraged him to change the venue and times of meetings and frequently to revise his travelling arrangements, often at the very last minute.

In September 1943, Stauffenberg was appointed to serve in the general army office, under General Friedrich Olbricht, a committed member of the Beck–Goerdeler group. Olbricht brought Stauffenberg into contact with the leading army figures involved in the plot to overthrow the Nazi regime.

The worsening military situation in 1944

The desperate military situation facing Germany became even worse after the successful landings of the Allied forces in Normandy on 6 June 1944. The D-Day landings, as they were known, were followed on 22 June 1944 by a blistering assault by the Red Army on the eastern front, which pushed the German army into a never-ending retreat.

In response to these critical developments, the Beck–Goerdeler group opened up talks with British and American diplomats in Switzerland concerning the possibility of an armistice, in the event of mounting a successful coup against Hitler, but these clandestine diplomatic overtures were flatly rejected.

Final attempts to win over the generals to the resistance struggle

In spite of this rebuff by the Allies, the Beck–Goerdeler group decided to go ahead with their plan to overthrow Hitler because many of the army resistance plotters believed that this act would help to restore some of Germany's tarnished reputation. As part of these plans, the Beck–Goerdeler group made a renewed effort to win support from the high command of the German army.

The most well known army figures already recruited by the army resistance group were Henning von Tresckow, a key figure in army group centre operating on the eastern front; Field Marshal Erwin von Witzleben, who was to have assumed the role of commander in chief of the armed forces had the coup against Hitler's regime been successful; and Major General Karl Heinrich von Stülpnagel, the military governor in German-occupied France.

The most well known new figure recruited by the army resistance during 1944 was Field Marshal Erwin Rommel, the 'Desert Fox', who had lost favour with Hitler following his defeat in North Africa during 1943. Rommel opposed the idea of killing Hitler, but was willing to support Goerdeler's idea of allowing Hitler to stand trial for his war crimes. The Beck–Goerdeler group made protracted overtures to persuade Field Marshal Günther von Kluge, the commander in chief of army group centre on the eastern front, to join the conspiracy. Kluge did express some sympathy towards the conspiracy, but gave no firm commitment.[3] Below the ranks of the army top brass, however, the Beck–Goerdeler group had more success and recruited a significant number of younger officers to support the resistance struggle.

The 'Valkyrie' plan

In July 1944, the Beck–Goerdeler group prepared detailed plans for military and political action to topple the Nazi regime. The crux of the plan (known as the 'Valkyrie' plan) was to assassinate Hitler. This was to be immediately followed by the issue of secret orders, which were designed to put down civil unrest. The orders were to be used (after Hitler's assassination) as a smoke screen designed to help the army seize control of Berlin and other key German cities. During the critical early hours of the proposed take-over of power, the Beck–Goerdeler group planned to seize the national radio station (which, in the days before television, was viewed as the major means of communicating information to the public) and to arrest all SS and Nazi national and local leaders. Once the army had gained control of Berlin, a state of martial law was to be declared. The temporary head of state was designated as General Beck, with Goerdeler assuming the role of Chancellor. The plans of the Beck–Goerdeler group, concocted in great secrecy, were very much of a piecemeal variety. In the event of Hitler's death, no one really knew what would actually happen.[4]

The launching of the assassination attempt on Hitler's life

Stauffenberg took central responsibility for the attempt on Hitler's life. He was determined to kill Hitler or be killed in the effort. In April 1944, Stauffenberg was appointed to serve General Friedrich Fromm, chief of general staff in the War Office, based in the Bendler Block, on Bendlerstrasse, in central Berlin. This high-profile post, serving the commander in chief of the German army, allowed Stauffenberg access to the military briefings of the Nazi dictator for the very first time.

At the beginning of July 1944, the plans for the conspiracy were finalised. Stauffenberg waited for a suitable opportunity to launch his attempt on Hitler's life. It finally came (after two aborted attempts) on 20 July 1944, while Stauffenberg was attending a military briefing, chaired by Hitler, at his heavily fortified and closely guarded military headquarters – the 'Wolf's Lair' at Rastenburg.

At 12.30 p.m. Stauffenberg left a bomb, with a 30-minute charged fuse, concealed in his briefcase, under a table, as near as he could place it to the Nazi dictator. Stauffenberg then sneaked out of the meeting and was driven by his personal assistant (Werner von Haeften) to a local airport, where they boarded a waiting plane, bound for Berlin, which took off at 1.15 p.m.

As Stauffenberg journeyed towards the German capital, he was convinced that Hitler had been killed in the explosion (which occurred at 12.45 p.m., resulting in four deaths and considerable damage). However, Stauffenberg did not know – or accept – until later in the evening that Hitler had miraculously survived the bomb blast with only minor cuts and burns.

The hours following the assassination attempt

At 3.45 p.m. on 20 July 1944 Stauffenberg's plane finally landed at Rangsdorf Airport, on the outskirts of Berlin. He travelled by car from the airport to the War Office in the Bendler Block. At 4.30 p.m. Stauffenberg walked into his office and immediately told his staff that Hitler was dead and the coup was under way. He immediately placed his boss, General Fromm, under house arrest.

In the four hours between the explosion going off at Rastenburg and Stauffenberg's arrival at the Bendler Block, there was a complete news black-out surrounding the attempt on Hitler's life. There was also great confusion in the German capital about what had happened. The first Valkyrie order (proclaiming a state of martial law) was not issued to general staff officers by Lieutenant General Friedrich Olbricht, a key figure in the conspiracy, until 3.45 p.m. However, loyal Nazi officers in Berlin became suspicious as to why General Paul von Hase, the Berlin city army commandant (who was part of the conspiracy),

Hitler showing Mussolini the room where he survived the bomb blast in 1944.

had ordered the army to take control of the capital without an order from the Führer. As a result, even after it was eventually issued, the first Valkyrie order, which was vital to the success of the revolt, was never carried out. No attempt was made to seize the radio station or to arrest leading Nazi ministers.

Meanwhile, General Beck, nominally the new head of state, arrived at the Bendler Block at 5 p.m. News was then relayed to the War Ministry which indicated that Hitler had been only slightly injured in the explosion. Stauffenberg rejected this news as Nazi propaganda.

At the same time, Joseph Goebbels, the Nazi Propaganda Minister, began a decisive Nazi counter-attack against the conspiracy from his government residence situated close to the Brandenburg Gate. Goebbels persuaded Major Otto Remer, whose Berlin guard units (equipped with steel helmets, hand grenades and submachine guns) had been ordered by Hase to take control of the key Nazi ministries, not to implement the order. In a telephone conversation between Remer and Hitler, the Nazi dictator ordered Remer to suppress the rebellion in Berlin. From this point onwards, Goebbels, supported by loyal German guard officers, was firmly in control of Berlin and the conspiracy was doomed. Hase was arrested on suspicion of treason. At 6.30 p.m. German national radio announced that Hitler had survived a bomb attempt on his life and would speak to the nation later in the evening.

Meanwhile, at the Bendler Block, Stauffenberg, in a series of desperate telephone calls, tried to persuade army officers throughout Germany to support the bungled insurrection. At 8 p.m. Witzleben, designated as the new supreme commander of the armed forces by the conspirators, finally arrived at the Bendler Block, declaring the day's events 'a fine mess'. Witzleben informed Stauffenberg that the conspiracy had failed and headed for home.

At 9.30 p.m. 200 members of the loyal Berlin guards battalion stormed the Bendler Block. After a short exchange of fire, Stauffenberg (who was wounded) and his four leading accomplices were placed under arrest. Beck immediately asked if he could shoot himself. He tried to do so twice, without success, before an army guard finally completed the grim task.

General Fromm was freed from house arrest and quickly convened a summary court-martial of the leading participants in the rebellion. He found the conspirators guilty of high treason and ordered their immediate execution. Stauffenberg took full responsibility for the conspiracy, but showed no regret or remorse for attempting to kill Hitler.

At midnight, Stauffenberg was led, with his three leading co-conspirators (Lieutenant General Friedrich Olbricht, Colonel Albrecht Ritter Mertz von Quirnheim and Lieutenant Werner von Haeften), downstairs to the courtyard of the Bendler Block, where all four were executed by a quickly assembled firing squad. Stauffenberg's last words were 'Long live Holy Germany'. The bodies of the four dead officers, and that of Beck, were unceremoniously bundled onto a lorry, which took them for burial at a cemetery in Schöneberg. On the next day, however, Heinrich Himmler, the head of the SS, ordered their bodies to be dug up, cremated and their ashes scattered in an open field.

The aftermath of the bomb plot

Outside Nazi Germany, there was little sympathy for those who had attempted to kill the Nazi dictator. The *New York Herald Tribune* wrote 'Let the generals kill the corporal [Hitler] or vice versa, preferably both.'[5] The London *Times* claimed that the generals who had led the bomb plot on Hitler's life were 'militarists' and no friends of liberty and democracy.[6] Winston Churchill told the House of Commons: 'The highest personalities in the Reich are murdering one another, or trying to, while the avenging armies of the Allies close upon the doomed and ever-narrowing circle of their power.'[7] It was widely believed outside Germany that the bomb plot on Hitler's life was part of a 'palace revolution' designed to salvage the power of the traditional German army elite from the ashes of Nazi militarism.

Inside Nazi Germany, the failed attempt on Hitler's life allowed the Nazis to completely destroy the complex network of conservative and military resistance groups which had grown up since the late 1930s. Hitler informed German radio listeners in the early hours of 21 July 1944 that a military coup by a 'clique of ambitious, unscrupulous and at the same time criminally stupid officers' had failed and would be dealt with in true Nazi fashion.

Henning von Tresckow, one of the leading generals involved in the conspiracy, committed suicide on the day after the bomb plot. All members of the Stauffenberg family – even distant relatives – were arrested and many of them were executed. Most of the leading German aristocratic families, many of whom had helped Hitler to gain power in 1933, were killed in the orgy of Nazi killing which followed the bomb plot.

The remaining figures involved in the plot were swiftly arrested by the Gestapo and brought before show trials in the notorious 'People's Court', presided over by Judge Roland Freisler, who humiliated the accused before sentencing them to death. A number of army officers implicated in the bomb plot were hanged in the most horrific manner imaginable: on meat hooks, suspended by piano wire.

On 22 August 1944, the SS launched 'Operation Thunderstorm', which led to the arrest of 5,000 former ministers and party officials from a wide variety of political persuasions, many of whom had no link at all to the bomb plot. On 22 December 1944, the Nazi regime announced the creation of 'National Socialist Leadership Officers', who would have control over the decisions of the German army. However, Hitler's very last order to the army high command in western Europe (the 'Nero Order'), which instructed the German army to destroy all industrial plants and machinery as they retreated, was never implemented.

The exact number convicted and executed in the aftermath of the bomb plot is not known, but as many as 5,000 opponents of the regime were executed or

The notorious Judge Freisler (centre) delivers a Nazi salute in court, with a bust of Hitler and a Swastika flag in the background. This picture was taken in 1944 at the opening of the trial that convicted the perpetrators of the July Plot.

murdered in connection with the failure of the assassination attempt on Hitler's life. Among those executed were Witzleben, Moltke, Hassell, Yorck and Canaris. Carl Goerdeler was arrested on 12 August 1944, but was not executed until 2 February 1945.

Document case study

20 July 1944: Stauffenberg and the bomb attempt on Hitler's life

6.1 A telegraph message sent from Field Marshal von Witzleben at the War Ministry to all military districts, at 4.45 p.m., 20 July 1944

The Führer Adolf Hitler is dead . . . In order to maintain law and order in this situation of acute danger the Reich Government has declared a state of martial law and has transferred the executive power to me together with the supreme command of the Wehrmacht [German army] . . . Any resistance against the military authorities is to be ruthlessly suppressed. In this hour of the greatest peril for the Fatherland the unity of the Wehrmacht and the maintenance of discipline is the most important requirement. I therefore make it the duty of all army, navy and air force commanders to support the holders of executive power with all means at their disposal and to ensure that their directives are obeyed by the agencies subordinate to them.

Source: J. Noakes (ed.), *Nazism 1919–1945: a documentary reader, vol. 4: The German home front in World War II*, Exeter, 1998, p. 621

6.2 A German radio broadcast, 10 p.m., 20 July 1944

For the second time in this war started by Jewry, a foul and murderous attempt has been made on our Führer's life . . . Providence protected the man who holds in his hands the destiny of the German people. The Führer remained unhurt . . . The fact that the Führer is alive is most important for us. The feeling of gratitude for his salvation is the supreme, the overwhelming emotion of all Germans. It finds its expression in the demonstrations of loyalty to and love for the Führer, which have already poured in from all over Germany. The German people will answer the cowardly attack on the Führer's life with a renewed profession of its allegiance to its National Socialist ideals, virtues and duties and with a solemn promise to fight even more fanatically and to work harder. 'With the Führer – to victory.' That is the slogan of the German people . . .

Source: Noakes (ed.), *Nazism 1919–1945, vol. 4*, p. 621

6.3 An eyewitness account by Otto John of the scene inside the Bendler Block in Berlin on the day of the bomb plot

In spite of the apparent turmoil, all I heard and saw, particularly in snatches of Stauffenberg's telephone calls, gave the impression that the whole Army was up in arms against the Nazis. It never occurred to me at that moment that they could reverse the process and stop everything . . . I had little doubt that Himmler would try and put up some resistance through the SS, but I was sure Hitler was dead . . . I left . . . at about 8.45 . . . So I went home to tell my brother what had happened at Rastenburg . . . We opened a bottle of champagne to drink to a glorious future. We were too excited to go to sleep and stayed up drinking champagne. We had the radio on, waiting for further news . . . Then, around one o'clock, Hitler spoke. It was unmistakably his voice. All our hopes vanished; we listened, breathless with sudden anxiety and bitter disappointment. What would happen now? I telephoned the Bendlerstrasse . . . But there was no reply. I realized they must have arrested Stauffenberg.

Source: R. Manvell and H. Frankel, *The July plot*, London, 1964, pp. 235–36

6.4 Adolf Hitler's speech to the German people, 1 a.m., 21 July 1944

My fellow German men and women! . . . I don't know how many attempts to assassinate me have been planned and carried out. But I am speaking to you today for two reasons, in particular: first, so that you can hear my voice and know that I am unhurt and in good health; secondly, so that you can hear the details of a crime for which there can be few comparisons in German history. A tiny clique of ambitious, unscrupulous and at the same time criminally stupid officers hatched a plot to remove me, and together with me virtually to exterminate the staff of the German High Command. The bomb, which was placed by a Colonel Count von Stauffenberg, exploded two metres to the right of me. It very seriously injured a number of loyal colleagues, one of whom has died [in fact, four people died in the explosion]. I myself am completely unhurt, apart from a very few minor grazes, bruises and burns . . . At a time when the German armies are engaged in a very tough struggle, a very small group . . . thought they could stab us in the back just like in November 1918. But this time they have made a very big mistake . . . The circle represented by these usurpers is extremely small. It has nothing to do with the German Wehrmacht . . . It is a very small clique of criminal elements, which will now be mercilessly exterminated . . . I would like to give to you, my old comrades in arms, a special greeting, glad that I have once more been spared a fate which had no terrors for me personally, but which would have brought terror to the German people. But I read into that the finger of fate pointing me towards the continuation of my work and so I shall carry on with it.

Source: Noakes (ed.), *Nazism 1919–1945, vol. 4*, pp. 624–26

6.5 The reaction of Henning von Tresckow, a leading member of the army resistance, to the failure of the bomb plot, 21 July 1944

The whole world will vilify us. But I am still firmly convinced we did the right thing. I consider Hitler to be the arch enemy not only of Germany but of the world. When, in a few hours, I appear before the judgement seat of God, in order to give account of what I have done and left undone, I believe I can with a good conscience justify what I did in the fight against Hitler . . . A person's moral integrity only begins at the point where he is prepared to die for his convictions.

Source: Noakes (ed.), *Nazism 1919–1945, vol. 4*, p. 618

1 Comment on the practicality of implementing the directive outlined in 6.1.

2 How does the radio broadcast, outlined in 6.2, depict those who participated in the assassination attempt on Hitler's life?

3 What insights does 6.3 provide about the attitudes of the resistance towards the bomb plot?

4 How does Hitler in 6.4 portray those who have attempted to overthrow the Nazi regime?

5 How does Tresckow, in 6.5, justify his own participation in the bomb plot?

Notes and references

1 See P. Hoffman, *Stauffenberg: a family history, 1905–1944*, Cambridge, 1995.

2 *Ibid.*, p. 152.

3 For a detailed analysis of Hitler's relationship with the German army high command, see H. Deutsch, *Hitler and his generals*, Minneapolis, 1974.

4 For a detailed study of the assassination plans for the July 1944 bomb plot, see H. Deutsch, *The conspiracy against Hitler in the twilight of war*, Minneapolis, 1968.

5 *New York Herald Tribune*, 9 August 1944.

6 *The Times*, 22 July 1944.

7 *The Times*, 3 August 1944.

7 The historical debate

The historical debate surrounding opposition and resistance in Nazi Germany has been intensely affected by the prevailing political climate in Germany.[1] It must be appreciated that until 1990, Germany was divided into the Communist German Democratic Republic (GDR) in the east, with a population of 17 million, and the liberal-democratic Federal Republic of Germany (FRG) in the west, with a population of 63 million. The division of Germany was a direct result of Germany's defeat in the Second World War and was symbolised by the Berlin Wall. This division greatly influenced the way in which German historians grappled with the legacy of the Nazi past. In East Germany, historians portrayed the Communist Party and its supporters as forming the most active resistance group facing the Nazi regime. In West Germany, historians viewed the elite conservative groups involved in the 1944 bomb plot against Adolf Hitler as the centre of anti-Nazi resistance. The unification of Germany in 1990, together with the ending of the Cold War, led to the historical debate over opposition and resistance in Nazi Germany becoming much less politically determined, with the result being a more open-minded discussion among German historians on the subject.[2]

The problems of definition

The definition of the term 'resistance' has always been a central issue of the historical debate. The problem with a too narrow definition is that it restricts study to the small elite which plotted to kill Hitler. On the other hand, a broad definition expands resistance to include even people who told mild jokes about the Nazis to friends.

Martin Broszat defined resistance as 'every form of rebellion' against the claim to total rule by the Nazi regime. This definition embraced a wide variety of actions, all displaying some rejection of Nazism, but most falling short of actually trying to overthrow the regime by force.[3] Broszat's wide-ranging definition of resistance has therefore been criticised by a number of historians, most notably Walter Hofer, who has claimed that only those actions which carried a clearly defined 'will to overcome' the Nazi regime should be classed as 'resistance'.

Another group of historians, including Heinz Boberach and Manfred Messerschmidt, have suggested that 'resistance' should be defined as those actions which the Nazi state and its police authorities defined as resistance.[4] Of course, the strength of such an approach means it is possible to examine what acts of defiance were regarded by the Nazi regime as the least through to the most dangerous.

Most historians would accept Detlev Peukert's view of a sort of pyramid model of 'resistance', beginning at the lowest and widest level with mild forms of 'nonconformity', such as telling jokes, rising up to embrace actual 'protest', including the spreading of rumours, to the highest point of 'political resistance', which involved acts of sabotage, conspiracy, the distribution of anti-Nazi literature, attacking Nazi organisations and trying to overthrow the regime by force. This pyramid structure of resistance fully recognises the difference between placing a bomb under Hitler's table, with the intention of killing him, and telling a close friend that Joseph Goebbels was a 'poison dwarf'.[5]

It does appear reasonable to reserve the term 'resistance' for those groups and individuals who made a determined and organised attempt to work against the regime in the hope of undermining it or planning its overthrow, and to use the broader term 'opposition' to explain actions and dissent from specific policies imposed by the Nazi regime but without a total rejection of the Nazi regime or a desire to take steps to overthrow it by force.

The bomb plot against Hitler in the historical debate

In early studies of German resistance there was a dominant concentration among West German, British and American historians on the small group of generals, conservatives and aristocrats involved in the 1944 bomb plot against Hitler. Hans Rothfels, the author of one of the first studies of the individuals and groups associated with the 1944 bomb plot, claimed that the leading figures in the conservative–military resistance – Stauffenberg, Goerdeler and Beck – were motivated by an ethical and moral hatred of Nazism and were also united in a desire to forge a new Germany based on principles of freedom and the rule of law out of the ashes of the Nazi regime.[6] The idea of the Beck–Goerdeler group as the forerunner of democracy in post-war West Germany soon became a common feature of the historical debate.

In more recent times, this traditional and generally favourable interpretation of the motives of the conservative–military resistance has been substantially revised. Hans Mommsen argues that the 'men of the 20th July' were not democrats but conservatives with a deeply ingrained mistrust of democracy, whose foreign policy aims included territorial expansion in eastern Europe and bitter hostility towards the Soviet Union.[7] According to Christian Streit, many of the leading generals involved in the bomb plot against Hitler also took part in the war crimes committed by the German army against Jews and Soviet prisoners of war during the invasion of the Soviet Union. It seems most of the leading figures in the military resistance were unconcerned about Nazi persecution of Communists and Jews.[8]

In their plans for government, the various conservative–military resistance groups wanted a strong army but they lacked any desire for the introduction of liberal democracy in post-war Germany. Hermann Graml has suggested that the leaders of the 1944 bomb plot against Hitler did not believe there was a need for the German army to suffer any loss of power in a post-war peace settlement, in spite of the fact that its tanks and planes had decimated most of Europe.[9] A great number of historians now believe the conservative–military resistance, which was led by servants of the Nazi state, withdrew support from Hitler's regime only because his type of nationalism became more extreme than their own version, which remained authoritarian, militaristic and anti-democratic. A moderate Hitler, pursuing limited territorial gains in eastern Europe, was fine. It was the out-of-control Hitler they did not like. With the exception of Stauffenberg, and some of the leading figures in the Kreisau Circle, there was very little love of democracy or any desire for fundamental political and social change.

The church struggle

Another key area of the historical debate is the resistance of the Christian churches against the Nazi regime. In early studies, the view that the churches mounted a principled stand in opposition to Nazism was widely accepted. In more recent studies, however, there has been a tendency for historians to suggest they were not as fundamentally opposed to Nazism as was previously thought. In fact, most of the leaders of the Protestant Church greeted the rise of Hitler in positive terms and they were also sympathetic towards the foreign policy, the anti-Communist and anti-Semitic aspects of the Nazi Party programme. According to Robert Ericksen, resistance to specific Nazi policies designed to restrict the right of the Protestant Church to govern itself was widespread, but outright resistance to the broad programme of Hitler's government was small.[10]

A majority of historians now accept that the 'church struggle' was primarily a matter of the Protestant Church trying to protect itself from Nazi domination rather than exhibiting any fundamental rejection of Nazi foreign, economic or social policies. Ericksen argues that resistance to Nazism did not characterise the Protestant Church, which rather struggled to retain independence from state control. Hence, the church struggle is now viewed by historians as an attempt by conservative forces in German society to oppose the creation of a totalitarian regime.

In recent studies of the Catholic response to the Nazi regime, it is also coming to be accepted that the hierarchy of the Catholic Church was likewise more obsessed with institutional survival than concerned to protect the victims of Nazism. Even so, most historians agree that Catholic opposition to the Nazi regime was a far more widespread phenomenon than existed within the Protestant Church. Donald Dietrich has recently shown that Catholic bishops did publicly attack Nazi 'master race' ideas and bravely denounced the Nazi euthanasia programme, which was aimed at the handicapped and mentally ill.[11] There is also evidence from Gestapo records that many Catholic priests were regarded as part of the resistance to the Nazi regime. Nevertheless,

Catholic opposition was primarily concerned with resisting Nazi claims to total control over German society rather than supporting the overthrow of the Nazi regime.

The broadening of the debate

In recent times, the historical debate has moved away from a narrow concentration on the elite resistance of generals, civil servants and pastors and priests towards the examination of resistance from broad sections of German society. The path-breaking 'Bavaria' research project on 'Resistance and persecution in Bavaria, 1933 to 1945', led by Martin Broszat, paved the way towards an examination of resistance to Nazism from a wide range of groups in German society. The Bavaria project showed there were numerous forms of civil disobedience against the Nazi regime.[12]

The Bavaria project also encouraged a greater interest in how the Communist Party had resisted the Nazi regime. In early studies by West German historians, the role of Communist and working-class resistance in general had been underplayed, dismissed or ignored. In more recent studies, it has now been accepted that Communists and workers played a very significant role in active resistance to the Nazi regime. The vast majority of those executed for engaging in political resistance listed their occupation as 'industrial worker'. Allan Merson, in a detailed study of Communist resistance in Nazi Germany, has shown that the great majority of those who took part in resistance activities against the Nazi regime were either Communists or manual workers.[13] Communist resistance is regarded by Merson as a moral triumph undertaken against overwhelming odds, and by Kershaw as a 'tragic failure' because the vast majority of the working class refused to support it. Indeed, the majority of the working class in Nazi Germany were neither rebellious nor posed a serious threat to the regime.

Another recent development in the historical debate on opposition and resistance in Nazi Germany is a great interest in the opposition by young people against the Nazi dictatorship. Detlev Peukert has recently shown how some young people expressed opposition to Nazi totalitarianism by organising illegal parties at which jazz and swing music was played and by forming youth gangs, such as the Edelweiss Pirates, who rejected the uniformity of the Hitler Youth. Indeed, Peukert has argued that the Edelweiss Pirates engaged in forms of behaviour which showed a complete rejection of National Socialism.[14]

The most poignant example of individual and ethical rejection of Nazism is the tragic but heroic stand taken by the university students in the White Rose group, who fought Nazism in order to defend individualism and personal freedom. According to J. P. Stern, the White Rose group, although they failed to make any dent in the Nazi regime, have achieved a subsequent immortality.[15] On the other hand, Kershaw suggests that the failure of the White Rose group shows the hopeless situation facing any individual or group which openly resisted the Nazi regime.[16]

Conclusion

In the final analysis, all types of resistance and opposition to the Nazi regime failed, because those people who bravely resisted Hitler actually numbered less than 1 per cent of the German population. We must remember that resistance to Nazism, although historically significant, never gained popular support from the German people, most of whom supported Adolf Hitler's attempt to make Germany the dominant power in Europe to the bitter end.

Notes and references

1 See E. Rosenhaft, 'The uses of remembrance: the legacy of the Communist resistance in the German Democratic Republic', in F. Nicosia and L. Stokes (eds.), *Germans against Nazism: nonconformity, opposition and resistance in the Third Reich*, Oxford, 1990, pp. 369–88.

2 For a detailed discussion of the historical debate on opposition and resistance, see I. Kershaw, *The Nazi dictatorship: problems and perspectives of interpretation*, 3rd edn, London, 1993, pp. 150–79.

3 *Ibid.*, p. 158.

4 *Ibid.*, pp. 160–61.

5 See D. Peukert, *Inside Nazi Germany: conformity, opposition and racism in everyday life*, London, 1987.

6 H. Rothfels, *The German opposition to Hitler: an assessment*, London, 1970.

7 See H. Mommsen, 'German society and the resistance to Hitler', in H. Mommsen (ed.), *From Weimar to Auschwitz: essays in German history*, Oxford, 1991, pp. 208–23.

8 See C. Streit, *Keine Kameraden: Die Wehrmacht und die sowjetischen Kriegsgefangenen 1941–1945*, Stuttgart, 1978.

9 H. Graml, H. Mommsen, H-J. Reichhardt and E. Wolf, *The German resistance to Hitler*, London, 1970.

10 R. Ericksen, 'A radical minority. Resistance in the German Protestant Church', in Nicosia and Stokes (eds.), *Germans against Nazism*, pp. 115–36.

11 See D. Dietrich, 'Catholic resistance to biological and racist eugenics in the Third Reich', in Nicosia and Stokes (eds.), *Germans against Nazism*, pp. 137–56.

12 See Kershaw, *The Nazi dictatorship*, pp. 157–58.

13 See A. Merson, *Communist resistance in Nazi Germany*, London, 1985.

14 See D. Peukert, 'Youth in the Third Reich', in R. Bessel (ed.), *Life in the Third Reich*, Oxford, 1987, pp. 25–40.

15 See J. P. Stern, 'The White Rose', in H. Siefken (ed.), *The White Rose: student resistance to National Socialism 1942–1943*, Nottingham, 1991, pp. 11–36.

16 I. Kershaw, 'Resistance without the people? Bavarian attitudes to the Nazi regime at the time of the White Rose', in Siefken (ed.), *The White Rose*, pp. 51–66.

Select bibliography

The available studies on resistance and opposition against Nazi rule are mostly specialised books and articles. The following list offers a selection of books on the key issues discussed in each chapter of the book.

General studies

The most useful introductory books on the subject are: M. Balfour, *Withstanding Hitler in Germany*, London, 1988; A. Gill, *An honourable defeat: a history of German resistance to Hitler*, London, 1994; H. Rothfels, *The German opposition to Hitler: an assessment*, London, 1970; and P. Hoffmann, *German resistance to Hitler*, London, 1988. There are a number of edited collections of essays which examine most of the issues discussed in this volume, most notably D. Large (ed.), *Contending with Hitler*, Cambridge, 1991; and F. Nicosia and L. Stokes (eds.), *Germans against Nazism: nonconformity, opposition and resistance in the Third Reich*, Oxford, 1990.

Specialist studies

There have been several studies of **Communist resistance**, most notably A. Merson, *Communist resistance in Nazi Germany*, London, 1985.

In recent years, a number of studies have examined **youth protest** inside Nazi Germany, most notably D. Peukert, *Inside Nazi Germany: conformity, opposition and racism in everyday life*, London, 1987.

The poignant story of the **White Rose group** is examined in H. Siefkin (ed.), *The White Rose: student resistance to National Socialism 1942–1943*, Nottingham, 1991.

There are a number of detailed studies of **opposition from the Christian churches**, most notably J. S. Conway, *The Nazi persecution of the churches 1933–1945*, London, 1968; and K. Scholder, *The churches and the Third Reich*, 2 vols., London, 1987, 1988.

There are several studies which deal with the **conservative and military opposition** inside Nazi Germany, including H. Deutsch, *The conspiracy against Hitler in the twilight of war*, Minneapolis, 1968; K. von Klemperer, *German resistance against Hitler*, Oxford, 1992; and R. Manwell and H. Fraenkel, *The Canaris conspiracy: the secret resistance to Hitler in the German army*, London, 1969. There are also many studies of the leading figures in the conservative and military resistance, including G. van Roon, *German resistance to Hitler: Count von Moltke and the Kreisau Circle*, London, 1971; G. Ritter, *The German resistance: Carl Goerdeler's struggle against tyranny*, London, 1958; and K-J. Müller, *General Ludwig Beck*, Boppard, 1980.

There have been a number of studies of Claus von **Stauffenberg** and the bomb attempt on Hitler's life in 1944, most notably P. Hoffmann, *Stauffenberg: a family history, 1905–1944*, Cambridge, 1995; and J. Kramarz, *Stauffenberg, the architect of the famous July 20th conspiracy to assassinate Hitler*, New York, 1967.

For a detailed examination of the **historical debate** regarding opposition and resistance, see Chapter 3 of I. Kershaw, *The Nazi dictatorship: problems and perspectives of interpretation*, 3rd edn, London, 1993, pp. 150–79.

Chronology

1933 *January:* Adolf Hitler appointed German Chancellor

February: Reichstag fire

March: Social Democrat members vote against the Enabling Act

June: All political parties, except the Nazi Party, are dissolved

July: Concordat signed between German government and the Vatican

July: The provincial Protestant churches are amalgamated to form a single 'Reich Church'

September: Martin Niemöller establishes the Emergency League of Pastors (which becomes known as the 'Confessing Church')

1934 *June:* 'Night of the Long Knives' – the blood purge of the SA (Nazi stormtroopers) and other political opponents of the Nazi regime

1935 *March:* The synod of the Protestant Church of the old Prussian union rejects the imposition of Nazi ideology in the Church

1936 *May:* Confessing Church leaders send a memorandum to Hitler denouncing the 'de-Christianising of German life' by the Nazi regime

1937 *March:* Pope Pius XI gives a speech entitled 'With Burning Concern', which denounces the Nazi regime for breaching the terms of the Concordat

March: 800 ministers of the Confessing Church are arrested and detained in concentration camps

1938 *May:* General Ludwig Beck writes a memorandum opposing Hitler's 'aggressive foreign policy'

August: Beck resigns as chief of the army general staff

September: Planned coup against Hitler, led by Beck, is called off following the signing of the Munich agreement

1939 *August:* The Soviet Union signs a non-aggression pact with Nazi Germany

September: Outbreak of the Second World War

November: Assassination attempt by Georg Elser on Hitler fails because the Nazi dictator arrives late at the Munich beer hall at which he is due to speak

1940 *January:* First plan for a new German constitution, in the event of Hitler's overthrow, is prepared by Carl Goerdeler and Ulrich von Hassell

1941 *June:* German attack on the Soviet Union begins

July: Catholic Bishop Clemens Graf von Galen denounces the Nazi euthanasia programme

1942 *May:* First meeting of the Kreisau Circle takes place

1943 *February:* The student resistance at Munich University, known as the 'White Rose', is discovered by the Gestapo and the leaders of the group – Hans and Sophie Scholl – are executed

March: A bomb left on Hitler's plane fails to explode

March: A secret memorandum from Goerdeler to leading army generals urges a coup against Hitler

August: The Kreisau Circle produces a constitutional programme for a post-Hitler Germany

October: Claus von Stauffenberg is appointed chief of staff in the general army office

1944 *January:* Helmuth James von Moltke and other leading figures in the Kreisau Circle are arrested

July: Bomb attempt by Stauffenberg on Hitler's life fails. Stauffenberg is executed by a summary court-martial only hours later. Beck, aided by a German officer, shoots himself. Henning von Tresckow commits suicide

August: Peter Graf Yorck von Wartenburg, a leading figure in the Kreisau Circle, is executed

September: Hassell is executed

1945 *January:* Moltke is executed

February: Goerdeler is executed

April: Admiral Wilhelm Canaris, Hans Oster and Pastor Dietrich Bonhoeffer are executed in Flossenbürg concentration camp

May: Second World War in Europe ends

Index

Index